# The Job Seeker Manifesto

# Resumes 3.0: Tools to Find Your

# Next Job!

By

Katherine Burik with Dan Toussant

The Interview Doctor®

Job Talk Press

Canton, Ohio

Paperback ISBN: 978-0-9893787-3-4

ePDF ISBN: 978-0-9893787-4-1

ePUB ISBN: 978-0-9893787-5-8

Copyright 2013 by Job Talk Press, an Imprint of The Interview Doctor, Inc.

Cover Design and Illustration by Justine Conklin
Book Design by Martha Fewell
Development Editing by Martha Fewell
Final Editing by Martha Fewell
Book Production by Bookmasters, Inc.

# The Job Seeker Manifesto

# Resumes 3.0:

# Tools to Find Your Next Job!

# DEDICATION – Katherine Burik

Writing a book is an adventure in organization, just like organizing a job search. While I know and love this subject very well, developing and organizing my thoughts in a way that enables readers to understand my vision has been a stretching and growing process. I hope the effort pays off.

Many people supported this effort. My husband, Kermit, put up with my energy and focuses on something other than him. My kids Marissa, Dan, and Brett let me practice on them. My sister Martha was willing to try something new. My coach, mentor, and friend Sherry Greenleaf pushes me at the right time.

My partner Dan Toussant is often the face of the business, freeing me up to write. Together we are taking The Interview Doctor to a new level.

## DEDICATION – Dan Toussant

The Interview Doctor partnership Katherine and I offer people wanting to make a job change or career change has been a real gift to both of us, and only possible because of you.

For all the candidates we have coached through the Interview Doctor, thanks for sharing your career planning and job-seeking challenges. Coaching is a teaching business, and when you teach, you learn at a deeper level; what we share in this book and the others to follow, we know – when it comes to job seeking: this is what works best.

To all of my family, especially Colleen, thanks for your strong support and your reliable love.

# About This Series: How to Read This Book

Finding a new job can be hard. It can also be a rewarding and enlightening experience. The difference is how you approach the search.

After talking to many candidates at The Interview Doctor and through our previous lives as human resource executives and recruiters in corporate America, we know candidates often share many of the same problems. We have some solutions that can help.

The key to a successful job search is to have a plan to distinguish yourself from other candidates. You have to be able to explain who you are or what you have to offer. Sadly, most candidates have absolutely no idea where to begin. While no one can figure that out for you, we can help guide you through the process.

The books in this series, The Job Seeker Manifesto, offers a step-by-step approach to finding a job including many strategies we learned from extensive experience throughout our careers. All the stories we share are true, reflecting real job seekers we worked with through The Interview Doctor. We changed the names to protect our clients' privacy.

This is the second book in a series addressing job search starting with 1) creating a strategic plan, then 2) creating the tools necessary to display your talents including resumes and your LinkedIn profile, and 3) strategically designing how you describe yourself starting with the critical question, "tell me about yourself".

Pick the topic or two that address your particular issue or read the entire series, depending on your specific needs and interests.

This second book provides you with a variety of tools you can use in your job search. The tools you choose should be appropriate for the kind of job you want. Not everyone will use the same tools and not everyone will use them in the same way. It depends on what you want.

Write in the margins. Take notes. Create worksheets. Challenge yourself to understand how to design tools that support your job search, tools that support your goals. Use the workbook, Resumes 3.0: Resume-in-a-Box Workbook, if you want more help.

Use these books to give yourself a head start over other candidates and find the job you love.

# Contents

# The Job Seeker's Manifesto:

# Resumes 3.0:

# Tools to Find Your Next Job!

# The Job Seeker's Manifesto:

# Resumes 3.0

You can often tell how old someone is by his or her perspective of resumes. In the "olden days", say 15 or 20 years ago, resumes - summaries describing an individual's last few jobs and education - were typed or printed on special fancy paper purchased from the local stationary store. Laid off employees might attend an outplacement workshop to develop a final resume. At the end of the day, they received 50 copies of their new resume, printed on nice paper to begin their job search. Then off went the prospective candidate to hand out resumes and find a job.

Young people reading this are muttering to themselves, "Typed?" "Fancy paper?" "Stationary store?" What the heck does that mean?

It is a sign of the times that things have changed so much so quickly. Business has changed. The world has changed. Resumes have changed too.

You no longer need to find a secretary to type your resume professionally. You do not need special paper from a special stationary store (translation: stationary = paper) to use exclusively for business purposes.

I still have printed copies of old resumes in my file cabinet. Maybe you do too. If you do, then you probably are one of the parents who advise their children to seek out a professional to write their resume. Those parents believe that a fancy, printed resume these days is the ticket to a new job; they still believe that resumes are static and must be professionally prepared.

Do not get me wrong. Part of our service is writing resumes for people. We are glad to do it. However, technology has changed the world. As a result, resumes have a different role in today's job search.

This book explores the new role of resumes in the 3.0 generation. Resumes are one of many tools required by job searchers. However, they are not necessarily the centerpiece of today's job search as they were in the past. Your job search is flexible; it is personalized to your interests. Therefore, to support that job search, your tools must be flexible as well. We will look at resumes as a part of the strategic toolbox you will assemble for your job search.

## Chapter 1

# What is a Resume?

"Resume" is a French noun meaning to continue. The job search resume is a description of your employment past and your goals for your employment future.

Since a job search is a continuation of employment from one employer or job to another it makes sense that, in your continuing career progression, you need tools to describe what you bring to the table from your past that will make you successful in the future.

The resume provides the rationale for a transition between old and new employment. Your experiences define you and support your future goals.

**Resumes Then**

In the old days, a resume was critical as the main way to tell people about you. Resumes used to be static, typed documents created and utilized in a manner that reflected the times. Professional secretaries typed resumes on a typewriter because that is what was available. Resumes were professionally printed on heavy bond paper that might have a nice watermark on it. We purchased extra sheets of the same paper to use for cover letters and matching mailing envelopes. We picked up the completed resumes at the stationary store or print shop in a clean brown bag where the resume stayed until you lovingly pulled one out to mail with a typed cover letter to people who might be interested in learning more about you.

If you were interested in two different areas, then you wrote up two different resumes. Changing these static resumes required retyping and reprinting. That meant getting it right the first time was very important. This kind of resume was the main method of presenting yourself and your experience to others in a position to hire you.

Not any longer. The world is different today.

Today almost everyone has a computer, knows how to type, and can print directly on a good printer in their home office. That means the ability to produce a resume on the spot has changed. The ability to type and print yourself means you can produce a resume custom designed to respond to the specific position available. Each resume can highlight specific experiences that correspond to the specific position. No more static printed resumes safely stored in a brown bags waiting for the proper moment.

In the days before social media, your resume was the only way to describe yourself to potential employers. If you wanted an employer to know about your background you gave them a written resume. There was nothing else. Today a paper resume may not even be necessary. You can easily get a job without a paper resume. There are so many more ways to tell your story.

## "Resume" Today

A resume remains a tool, part of your strategic personal marketing plan. However, the old paper resume is only one of many tools at your disposal to share your background and experiences with potential employers.

We use the word "resume" loosely these days. A resume is not just a written document.

A resume can be paper or virtual now. A virtual resume allows you to expand beyond the margins of two sheets of fancy bond paper to tell the reader what you want and why you should have it. It is another way to tell your story. This new kind of "resume" is a consistent reflection of the person you want people to see whether they encounter you in social media outlets like LinkedIn or Facebook or meet you in person at a networking event or in a formal interview with a paper resume in your hand.

We usually start creating your "resume" with the actual paper resume. Today almost everyone has a computer, knows how to type, and can print directly on a good printer in their home office. That means the ability to produce a resume on the spot has changed. The ability to type and print yourself means you can produce a resume custom designed to respond to the specific position available. Each resume can highlight specific experiences that correspond to the specific position. No more static printed resumes safely stored in a brown bags waiting for the proper moment. The ability to change the focus of your experience, and the discipline of editing your experiences down to a one or two page format helps identify the most important information to support your goals. LinkedIn and social media options flesh out more details that might not be included in the paper document.

# Chapter 2

## What do you stand for?

Your "resume" is a sum of the information available about you that you use to draw a picture of the "you" that you want to show to the world. It should be a reflection of your brand. Every word should be, carefully planned for its strategic ability to highlight your strengths and make you look like the perfect candidate for the job you want. Tailor your resume to the specific job you want.

It is interesting to think of yourself as a "brand". Let's play a little game. What image comes into your head when you hear these names?

- Coke
- Apple

- Starbucks
- Kleenex
- Xerox

Does Coke make you think a brown carbonated drink? The brand name, "Coke," is so strong that in some parts of the southern United States the term "Coke" means any cold soft drink. The server will say, "What kind of Coke would you like?" You can even answer "Pepsi" if you want. They still call it "Coke."

Apple brands are so strong it seems like "i" anything will sell. We have iPhones, iPods, and iTVs. We have confidence that "i" products come with the Apple brand strength.

Starbucks means good coffee to me, a great place to sit and talk to friends. The name is instantly recognizable.

Kleenex and Xerox stand for flimsy paper to blow your nose in and a machine to make copies, respectively. Every company that makes tissue paper and copy machines tries to overcome the challenge but in most people's minds tissue paper and copy machines are Kleenex and Xerox.

Why is a name so strongly associated with a product that an image immediately pops into your head? That is the power of a brand.

These companies work hard to have a consistent brand. That instant name recognition comes after plenty of up front work. Consistent product design and quality contribute to the impression they want customers to have. Constant repetition makes you associate the name with the product. The 'also-ran' brand does not stand a chance. Every other variation falls away. We can picture these products in our minds. Nothing else will do.

You cannot have a great brand with an awful product. However, you can have a great product that no one ever looks twice at if it does not have a strong brand.

### What is your brand?

When someone says your name, wouldn't it be nice if your name summoned an instant, positive message to mind?

When someone says, "Katherine Burik" I want that name to be synonymous with a friendly, energetic, expert business coach. When someone says, "Dan Toussant," it would be great if the name meant knowledgeable, helpful, experienced recruiter and coach.

We want to be known as smart business people, capable of providing good advice based on our experience. Our main job is to make people know that we are the best at what we do so that when they think about job search or interview coaching, I want the first name they think of to be mine.

I do that by working on my brand. I want people to have a positive impression of the work I can do and the experience I create for my clients. My brand includes my past work and the reputation I create based on what other people think about my work and me.

Your challenge as a job seeker is to create a great brand. Your resume and other search tools as well as the stories you choose to tell about yourself should support your brand.

**Broadcast your "brand"**

Your LinkedIn profile is the foundation upon which you build your brand. All other tools such as your paper resume, business cards, and stories you tell can be structured around your LinkedIn profile giving your brand a consistent theme.

Think of your experience as your little black dress, or for men a basic black suit. When I wear a little black dress, I use jewelry or accessories to change the look slightly to suit my purpose. Men change the look of their dark suits with different color or style shirts or ties to fit in with the occasion. Your basic profile is like your little black dress. You can dress it up or down by emphasizing aspects of your experience that enhance your qualifications for the position you seek.

If your brand is the sum of all your experience, you can highlight the aspects of your experience that support what you want in the same way Coke offers different aspects of itself to the marketplace. Diet Coke is still Coke. iPhone is still Apple. Each is a subset of the master brand. The parts of your experience you choose to highlight are still part of your brand. They are the portions you want to emphasize now because it suits your purpose, just like Diet Coke or choosing a red tie over a blue tie.

The paper resume document can be the first step in your job search. You might start your job search by preparing a paper resume because it is what you are used to or because it is easier to prepare the resume elements on paper. However, a paper resume is not the end or even the main tool.

The core question is not how to write a resume but how to create a consistent, positive brand or reputation then share your brand with others. Use the process of writing a resume to understand and position your brand then extend that brand into social media so viewers can get a consistent impression of who you are and what you offer to employers.

Once you understand your brand, you can format a resume available in paper and electronic versions. Each has different purposes but both start with the same concepts.

So, let us look at the resume as an exercise in identifying your brand. Once we put together a good-looking resume that describes you well, we will explore how to put that information into your LinkedIn profile then build your brand or reputation around it.

**Electronic job searching**

Resumes have changed because job search has changed. Finding a job today depends on social media. LinkedIn provides an electronic "home base" where your electronic resume lives. Your LinkedIn profile, or electronic resume, works for you while you are sleeping. People will find you by searching this electronic resume for the key words and experiences you choose to include that make you desirable for the job you want.

Think of it like a big electronic dating game. Like Match.com for employers. A hiring manager (could be someone in human resources, a recruiter who finds people for a living, or the person who is hiring some-one for his or her team) identifies certain characteristics needed for the job then goes to the electronic store that is LinkedIn to find someone who meets those specific needs.

Your LinkedIn profile stands there holding your space while you are off networking and meeting peo-ple who can help. Hiring managers are shopping for new talent at the same time you are shopping for a new position. Your electronic resume in the form of your LinkedIn profile remains there and says, "Hello, I am Katherine and this is my brand. This is who I am. Let's talk about how we can help each other."

**Using Social Media**

According to the SHRM Research Spotlight, 56% of companies surveyed use social medial to recruit poten-tial candidates in 2011. Social media refers to sites like LinkedIn, Facebook, Twitter, or any type of virtual in-terpersonal communication that enables persons to in-teract online. This is a significant increase since 2008 when a little over one-third (34%) of organizations were using these sites. The most popular social networking website in 2011 was LinkedIn at 95%, followed by Facebook at 58% and Twitter at 42% (Society for Human Resource Management, 2011).

The top reason organizations cited for using social networking websites in recruiting was to "recruit passive job candidates who might not otherwise apply or be contacted by the organization", cited by 84% of respondents (Society for Human Resource Management, 2011). This is critical. Employers are out there shopping for candidates who might not even know they are candidates. You want the best representation of you and your brand visible when they come to look at you.

What does your LinkedIn profile say about you? You need to look with a critical eye. Better yet, ask someone else to look at your profile and tell you what your profile says about your brand.

We meet plenty of people in the course of our networking who say they do not really pay attention to LinkedIn because they are not searching for a job at that moment. How silly! Imagine the opportunities they are missing by having an incomplete or sloppy LinkedIn profile! Hiring managers are out there every day looking for talented people for open positions or for future needs. You want to make connections whenever an opportunity arises, whether you are looking or not.

Keep your LinkedIn profile up to date and a solid representation of your brand so you do not miss any opportunities. Let your LinkedIn profile work for you.

**Flexibility and Versatility**

Your brand is the way you describe your reputation and goals but it is not static. You can adjust the way you describe yourself to appeal to the kind of job you want.

For example, my brand as a friendly, energetic, expert coach is based on years of human resource experience. People I have worked with or interacted with over the years have seen a portion of me. People I meet now see the experience I choose to show them. All these views go into my overall brand. I can demonstrate my friendly, energetic expertise in many ways depending on my audience and depending on what I want people to see. My human resource experience is broad enough so I can define myself in a number of ways depending on what I want and what I believe the people I meet want to see.

If I wanted a position as a human resource executive, I could highlight different experiences that correspond to the experiences desired by any given company. I could highlight my experience with talent development in a company that believes that to be important or my employee relations experience in a company that believes employee issues to be their particular challenge. I am still the same person with the same brand. Highlighting different aspects of my experience broadens my opportunities.

Your bottom line goal is to find a position. Define your brand and use it to your advantage to expedite your job search. This expands your opportunities to fit your experience to more situations.

I think you need to remind us that Book 1 helped us define what we wanted to be. Here we are going to identify everything we are capable of and determining how to best highlight or feature those to find the job we want to have.

# Chapter 3

## Make your resume work

Making your professional information widely available online does not negate the need for a paper resume. The paper resume still has value as a way of focusing the interesting bits about you in one place, for example as a reference point during face-to-face meetings. A good-looking resume, saved electronically, gives you both paper and electronic versions.

While many different people can be looking at your resume, the largest numbers will fall into one of two categories.

- Hiring managers are functional managers who have a vacancy on their team that they would like to fill. Sometimes hiring managers use human resource professionals to screen resumes and sometimes they screen resumes themselves.

- Recruiters can work inside the company in the human resource department or they can be professionals who work independently on behalf of a company to identify candidates for specific openings.

You can never be certain who will be looking at your resume. It does not really matter anyway. Both categories of resume readers represent employers with vacancies that might be perfect for you. Your virtual or paper resume needs to appeal to both.

Employers (recruiters or hiring managers) use the paper resumes in several ways:

*To hold a space* –they might keep certain resumes as a way of remembering which people they like for a particular position that is open now or might be open in the future

*To share information about people they want to remember* – they can share a resume with other people inside or outside the company who might have an interest in someone with that background

*As a notepad* – they might mark portions of a paper resume with a highlighter to indicate areas to probe or remind them of questions they want to ask

*As a prompt* – a method of recalling an individual's background, basic facts, and accomplishments when meeting a candidate for the first time

Be sure to bring a paper resume with you when you go to a job interview. The people you are meeting almost certainly have seen your electronic resume or your LinkedIn profile. However, do not assume that they have that information in front of them when you arrive.

Hiring managers are notoriously underprepared for interviews. You will seem prepared and organized if you have several paper resumes in your portfolio to save some harried hiring manager the hassle of finding your resume from the stack of paper on his or her desk or in an electronic file in his or her computer. Being prepared with a paper resume can enhance your professional image.

You could also tuck a paper resume in your portfolio when you meet people for coffee or have information or networking meetings. You cannot assume that the people you are meeting know much about you or read the electronic attachment you sent earlier. Being able to slip a paper resume across the table makes you look organized and prepared.

**Use a Familiar Format**

You might think your resume perfectly identifies all that you are capable of doing. However, what good is it if hiring managers will not read it?

Your resume should provide information that employers (either recruiters or hiring managers) need in the manner and fashion that employers want to see it. If it does not, it will be discarded. Employers will not spend time on resumes that do not immediately attract their attention or answer their questions.

In the past, people believed folks spent a few minutes reading resumes. This was well accepted. As a person who used to hire people, I thought for sure I spent at least a minute or two on each resume.

A study by *The Ladders* finds that professional recruiters spend only 6 seconds on average on each resume they read (Evans, 2012). Count out six seconds. It is almost no time at all.

In a quantitative study of professional recruiters' behavior using a technique called "eye tracking," the study measured recruiters' eye movement while they read resumes. Recruiters' have a consistent method of reading resumes. The study indicated that recruiters spend almost 80% of their reading time looking at name, current title/company, previous title/company, start and end dates, and education. Then they scanned for keywords matching the open position. They want to see the information laid out in a consistent fashion so it is easy to read in a familiar manner. The most shocking thing of all:

**Everything else was irrelevant!**

*The Ladders'* study gives us insight into where you should focus your energy (Evans, 2011). Make sure your resume is easy on the eyes with critical information readily available, plenty of keywords at the top of the resume. Other details had little impact on the initial decision maker.

Do not just use more words. Instead target your words directly to what employers want to see, organized in a manner that employers want to see it.

The Ladders' study concludes that simple profiles are the best. Professional resume writers can help because they offer an organized, easy to read layout that makes it easier for recruiters to do their jobs.

Make sure your resume is an easy to read, strategic tool to get the most attention to what you have to offer. Keep it simple, well organized, and easy to read.

## Give yourself every advantage

Hiring managers who are looking to fill a position are under a lot of pressure. They have a vacancy on their team that they are trying to fill so they are understaffed. Everyone does extra work in the meantime until the manager fills the position, putting extra pressure on the manager to deliver results without adequate staff to do the work. Therefore, hiring managers are likely doing the work themselves. Recruiting to fill vacancies at the same time they are trying to get everything else done is a huge headache.

Consequently, candidates think hiring managers are rude and indifferent. Hiring managers are frustrated that recruiting takes so long when all they want is the right candidate to step out of the (literal or figurative) pile of resumes and fill the void. It is an awful situation all around.

Give yourself an advantage by making your resume easy to read and making shows that you have what the hiring managers need.

**Translate your experience**

A hiring manager must be able to look at your resume and see what they need translated in their terms. The information on your resume must mean something to the hiring manager. You could be the perfect candidate for a job but if the hiring manager does not quickly see that, you are out.

### Steven's Experience

Steven was an engineer who went back to school for an MBA to transition to a career in marketing. His resume reflects his engineering experience, naturally, since he previously worked as an engineer. He wrote his resume from the point of view of an engineer, highlighting what is important to engineers. He was an engineer so this made sense. However, engineers have different experiences and expectations than marketing people.

Steven's engineer-oriented resume did not get any attention for the marketing job he wanted in his new career. He was disappointed about this job search stall. He knew he needed a different perspective. If he wants a position in marketing he needs to translate his experience into terms that marketing people can understand.

Marketing people do not think they want to hire engineers. They want to hire people who are capable of understanding how a product (designed and produced by engineers) can appeal to customers. An engineer like Steven will add a lot of value to the marketing department because he understands product development from the inside, since he used to be an engineer. His resume needs to explain this value to hiring managers.

Steven's engineering experience offers very positive parallels for the marketing job he wants next.

- As an engineer, Steven worked on big projects, just like marketing people.
- Steven developed new products. In some companies, marketing teams drive new product development.
- Steven brings strong project management skills and experience on cross-functional teams that would make some marketing department very successful.
- As an engineer, Steven worked with vendors and was actively involved in product quality: important elements to marketing departments involved in product development.

We changed Steven's resume to highlight his prior involvement in big projects, new product development, cross functional teams, vendor relations, and quality improvement in a way that marketing folks will understand. Only then did hiring managers understand how Steven could be an asset to a marketing department. With these changes in his profile and resume, Steven got a marketing job.

You need to describe your experiences in terms that hiring managers can understand. Translate if necessary. Research advertisements for the positions you want. What words pop up consistently in those ads? What position expectations and requirements pop up consistently?

Those words and phrases are more than hints. Hiring managers are directly telling you what they want to see. It is your job to translate your experiences into words and phrases corresponding to what the hiring manager is looking for. We never lie or exaggerate but we can display our experiences to be most appealing to those who are looking for someone to hire. This helps everyone.

# Building a Resume

## Do it yourself vs. Professional

### Penelope's Experience

> Penelope was returning to the workforce after a three-year break to care for her dying mother. She took this opportunity to change careers. For many years, she volunteered with large charitable groups in her community like Junior League and fundraisers for the local children's hospital. She loved organizing events. The events she organized came in on budget and raised lots of money. She wanted to turn that experience into a career as an event planner.

*When she contacted The Interview Doctor, she said she contracted with another firm to write her resume but nothing was happening in her job search. She thought the resume might be the problem. I looked.*

*Penelope's resume was awful. This two-page resume not only looked ugly with its tiny font and squishy margins, but everything could easily have fit on one page. Worse, the resume did nothing to sell Penelope's skills as an event planner. What could we do to help?*

Usually people ask for help with their resume when their job search takes an inordinately long time. They think the resume must be the problem. Helpful "experts" offering conflicting suggestions about how to adjust a resume often confuse new clients.

We believe a professional can help. Nevertheless, a professional cannot do it all. Never ask a professional to write the entire resume for you. There are specific things that a professional *CAN* do for you. For example, a professional *CAN* help you:

- Assemble information into a format that meets your job search needs.
- Translate experiences into language employers understand.
- Save you hours of frustration by taking editing your resume and changing it to meet your goals better.

On the other hand, a professional *CANNOT*:

- Know what you have done or what your stories are. Only you know your experiences.
- Find you a job. You need to understand clearly what you want and where you can find it. You must find your own job.

A professional can help you prepare tools and can make those tools look great but the guts of the job search comes from you.

Our advice is to build a resume yourself then seek help for formatting and presentation. It will save you hours of time and be a more successful representation of your skills and experiences for the job you want.

Sadly, Penelope's situation is not unique. Different resume professionals have different points of view about what a resume should look like. I happened to think Penelope's resume was ugly. Clearly, another resume writer thought it looked fine. Only two opinions count: Penelope's and the hiring managers. Since Penelope did not like the resume and it was getting no traction from hiring managers, it was clear we had a problem. We kept the words the former resume writer used but reorganized everything to suit the branding needs of an event planner. With the revised resume, Penelope started to get traction with her job search.

**Why "build" a resume?**

When an architect builds a house, she starts with a goal. She has to understand how the owners will use the house in order to provide the design elements the owner will need.

The house should accomplish a certain purpose.

- If it will be a home to a family with children, then it needs several bedrooms, maybe a few bathrooms and a playroom.

- If it will be a home for a couple, then it might have fewer bedrooms but more space for entertaining.
- If it will be a home for an elderly person, it might need to be on one floor with wider halls in case the owner needs a wheel chair or walker.

Begin planning your resume similarly – with the end in mind. This way, you can choose the materials that make sense to accomplish the goal. Just as the "green" architect makes conscious choices of one material over another, you need to select and focus on the best items to achieve your goal.

With your career goal as a focus, you can tell that not every professional experience will receive the same attention because not every experience is relevant to your goal. You only highlight the experiences that support your goal.

Now it is time to inventory your skills, experiences, and abilities. Think about your past experiences, your interests, who you are and the way you work. Then select the details that support your goal.

## Identify your Goals

Define what you want very clearly. No one can do that for you. A professional cannot tell you what you want. Only you can.

Ask yourself:

- What gives you passion?
- What is the best use of your skills for the most reward?

At the intersection of your passion and the best use of your skills is the job that will make you happy. There should be a relationship between your background and your goals.

I might say I want to be a professional musician but my lack of training and lack of basic talent makes that impossible. I could search all I want for jobs as a professional musician but I will not succeed.

However, my background makes human resources a natural fit for me. I understand how to work with executives to achieve business goals. I listen well. People like to talk to me. I like to solve problems with people. The human resource experience makes me a good coach. I like being a coach so it is nice that my background and interests fit so well in my current job.

### Carrie's Experience

*Carrie has been searching for a new job for a few months and not getting anywhere. The only response she got to her resume was from insurance companies and financial services companies who want her to sell on full commission. Those kinds of companies will hire anyone because the burden is on the individual. Carrie does not want to sell insurance or financial services. She has a health care background with training in medical records – this is a valuable experience set in the current market since hospitals and physicians are converting to electronic medical records.*

*Unfortunately, Carrie is desperate. She tells anyone who will listen that she will do anything. Consequently, her job search has been scattered. She*

*asked The Interview Doctor to look at her resume,*
*thinking her resume must be the problem.*

A cursory look at her resume revealed a number of formatting problems and an unattractive resume. This, however, was not the reason her job search stalled. The biggest obstacle to her job search was that she did not know what she wants. She did not have a goal. Without a goal, it is not possible to translate her background in medical records, insurance, and hospitals into something that employers might want. Therefore, her resume was just a jumble of words. No employers were willing to wade through the mess on her resume to help her fit in.

We can fix format issues with the resumes easily enough. That is just the start, though. Cosmetic adjustments to the resume will not cover up the fact that Carrie did not know what she wants.

The Job Search Marketing Plan, the first book in The Job Seeker Manifesto series, might help Carrie. That book discusses in detail the steps to take to decide what you want to do.

Carrie can begin by researching the job ads to see what jobs kinds of positions that she finds appealing. She needs to read as many as it takes with as many different titles as possible. She is doing research, not preparing to apply for jobs.

She figured out that the jobs in health care marketing and consulting where she could help medical practices convert to electronic medical records would be a great fit for her skills and interests. This is a great idea for Carrie. Her background, experiences, and interests converge on this kind of position.

With this information, we structured a resume that looks great and highlights Carrie's background to support her goal. Her job search took off!

## Exercise 1: Identify your goal

1.  Go to online job listings in Monster.com or Indeed.com, a service that consolidates job ads posted in many different places on the Internet. Remember you are doing research not submitting resumes for any particular job.

2. In the "search" box, type in the kind of job you are looking for. Enter as many key words describing the kind of work you think you would like to do as you can think of. Do not limit yourself to a particular geography. Since you are not actually applying for the job, it does not matter where the job is located. This is research, not the opportunity to apply for jobs.

3. Read many job descriptions until you find the jobs that really sound great. Use variations of the job title in the search box until you find jobs that sound perfect for you.

4. Identify four or five "dream" jobs. These jobs could be perfect for you. Do not worry about details like experience or location.

5. What are common elements among those dream jobs?

6. Distill the title of the dream jobs into a few words. This is your headline, your job search goal.

**What to include**

Carrie's original resume included every job she held since she left college. She changed jobs frequently and changed industries three times. Does she include everything? How does she know what is important and what is not important?

**Exercise 2: Responsibility Inventory**

- At the top of the sheet of paper, list your goal, your ideal job. This is your headline.

- Create an Inventory - List every professional responsibility you can remember every having whether it seems related to your goal or not. Begin by listing every job and identifying your responsibilities in that position. Nearly every job position includes multiple responsibilities so think carefully. It may be useful to think about the things you do or did on a daily basis. Include everything. You will edit it later.

**Job 1:** _____

Responsibility 1: _____

Responsibility 2: _____

**Job 2:** _____

Responsibility 1: _____

Responsibility 2: _____

### An Honest Use of Facts

Tell the truth – we never lie or even exaggerate. Ever. It is just not worth it. It is possible to find countless stories of famous folks who lied about their background, then regretted the poor choice when they were caught.

An MIT dean never received any college degrees despite claiming to have a bachelors and master's degree. A former Notre Dame head coach lied about a master's degree and having been a football legend in college when he never actually played football. Yahoo's former CEO never earned the computer science degree he claimed. The Washington DC school superintendent who resigned after allegedly falsifying test results but now touts the results from the falsified tests as if no one will notice (Giang and Lockhart, 2012).

Surveys by Accu-Screen, Inc. ADP, and The Society of Human Resource Managers (2004) reveal some sad statistics:

- 53% of resumes and job applications contain falsifications
- 70% of college students surveyed would lie on a resume to get a job they wanted
- 78% of resumes are misleading

It is at best unnecessary and at worst dangerous to lie, falsify, or exaggerate your accomplishments on your resume.

Most employers check references and education. It is pretty easy to spot the lies. The damage to your reputation and brand can be permanent. It is so much easier to tell the truth.

It is ok to tell the truth from your perspective or the portions of the truth that support your story. It is never acceptable to lie or exaggerate.

### Stan's Story

> *Stan was terminated in a big conflict with his boss who was a bully. It would be better to avoid discussing the gory details of the conflict.*

*The fix*: Stan needs a short, plausible explanation that does not go into the details. He could say, "My boss and I had philosophical differences and agreed that it would be better if I left." This is true. With a statement like this, Stan can avoid going into the gory details.

### Kayla's Story

> *Kayla took a job only to discover she hated it. She just never clicked with the people or the work itself. She found another job a few months later. Should she put the short assignment on her resume?*

The fix: If the assignment was not significant, she should leave the short assignment off the resume. It just takes up space and raises questions.

## Changing Titles

In my last company, "Leader" was an important title. Every department had "leaders" of this and that. However, that means nothing to the outside world. A person holding a "leader" title would need to translate that title into one that means something. The Finance Leader was actually a Finance Manager in the outside world. Change the title so that someone in another company can understand your role.

It is perfectly acceptable to translate titles to make your experience more understandable to a hiring manager. That does not mean you can say you were a Vice President when you were an assistant. Nevertheless, if your title is confusing or is specialized to a particular company then you almost have to change the title so people outside the company will understand. Otherwise, you risk having your resume discarded in favor or someone else with a more easily understood background.

We never lie or exaggerate but we can clarify and simplify to aid understanding and acceptance.

**Facts and Figures**

You would be shocked at the resumes we see missing important information. In any given day, a hiring manager will even see resumes without critical contact

information like telephone numbers or email address-
es. What does that kind of oversight say about the candidate?

Make a list of all the important information. Do not
skip anything. You can always edit. Here is a partial
list of basic information to include in your resume, in
addition to work experience:

- Name
- Address, city, state and zip code
- Telephone number – include the phone number
  you use the most; most people include a cell
  phone number
- Email address
- College attended – you might leave the year off
  your paper resume if you graduated 10 years
  ago or more although it will appear in your
  LinkedIn profile. If you went to several schools
  before you graduated consider whether you
  want to include all those schools or only the
  school where you receive the degree. (Tradition-
  ally, it is only appropriate to list the degree-
  granting institute.)

- Degree received and major

- Anything special about your college experience that supports your goal – GPA if it is good and you are a recent grad, or scholarships, honors or special recognition like graduating with honors like cum laude, Phi Beta Kappa, or Rhodes Scholar. We advised a recent younger client to include National Merit Scholar Winner from high school on his post college resume because it is so impressive.

- Certificates and Credentials relating to your goal –Dan and I include on our resumes that The Society of Human Resource Managers certified us as Senior Professional Human Resource (SPHR) professionals because this important recognition enhances our credibility. Other people might include CPA, insurance licenses, nursing licenses or other certifications related to the work they do.

- Associations – list the groups you belong to that relate to your goal; exclude religious or political associations unless those organizations related directly to your goal. If you are in politics, you will include your political affiliations. Otherwise, leave it off even if it is a big focus of yours.

## Exercise 3: Your Responsibilities

Describe each responsibility for each job. You may have more than one Responsibility for any given job. List them all for now. Then consider whether that responsibility relates to your goal.

**Job 1:** _____

    **Responsibility 1:**_____

    _____

    **Does it relate to my goal?**

    **Responsibility 2:**_____

    _____

**Does it relate to my goal?**

**Responsibility 3:**_____

_____

**Does it relate to my goal?**


**Job 2:** _____

**Responsibility 1:**_____

_____

**Does it relate to my goal?**

**Responsibility 2:**_____

_____

**Does it relate to my goal?**

**Responsibility 3:**_____

_____

**Does it relate to my goal?**

If these responsibilities do not relate to your goal then they might not be important to include in your resume.

Look critically at the responsibilities you identify as related to your goal and what are not. Do you see any patterns? Which past roles should you emphasize? Should some be de-emphasized? This is important information for creating your resume.

What patterns am I looking for? What do you mean by patterns? Examples?

Even though your resume will be a chronological listing of the jobs you have held, you highlight the experiences that contribute to explaining who you are and what you want – experiences that support your target job.

### Lila's Story

*Lila is a sales manager for a large electronics distributor. She has a successful record of accomplishment of inside and outside sales. She wants to update her resume because she is afraid her job is at risk.*

*Her resume and LinkedIn profile were not bad. She has a nice picture and all the required LinkedIn elements to get started: a decent number of contacts and groups. She had highlighted the skills that would get her attention as a sales manager.*

*Nevertheless, Lila does not want to be a sales manager any longer. She wants to be a trainer. She loves to create curriculum and design and deliver training programs that support leaders' efforts to grow and business's efforts to improve profitability. This information was neither present nor visible in her current resume.*

After long discussions about her responsibilities, we could see that Lila was a very good trainer. She has plenty of experience and plenty of demonstrated results. However, the job titles and experiences she chose in her current resume supported sales management, not training.

Lila told us about the training programs she created and delivered, identified the problems that those programs addressed, and described the results achieved by the people she trained. All this information supports her skill and justifies her transition into a new field. Once we identified this information, the resume was easy to transform.

- We put Lila's titles, jobs, and dates in chronological order.
- We inserted her goal, Training Director, at the top of the resume so everyone looking at the resume could see Lila wanted a position as a Training Director.
- We adjusted all bullets describing Lila's accomplishments to reflect achievements from training she delivered rather than her sales achievements. We did not discuss her sales results because those results are no longer relevant to her chosen role as Training Director.

Remember Steven who wanted to change from engineering to marketing? His final resume listed the jobs he held in chronological order but the accomplishments and words used to describe his jobs were words appropriate for a marketing position.

Which of your daily responsibilities represent you in the way you want to be known in your next role?

I have many years as a Human Resource executive. If my target job were to be Vice President of Human

Resources in a company that had challenges in em-ployee relations, I would highlight my employee rela-tions experiences and accomplishments and downplay other experiences. If my target job had the same title but I wanted to focus on talent development, I would highlight different experiences and accomplishments. The resumes would have the same chronological histo-ry but the responsibilities and accomplishments might be completely different. The resume becomes a strate-gic tool that makes me look great for either position, depending entirely on my goal.

**Responsibilities vs. Accomplishments**

Aside from typographical errors, one of the worst ways to mess up your resume is to focus on responsibilities instead of accomplishments. Building a resume may start with identifying responsibilities but it does not stop there. A good resume goes beyond responsibilities to demonstrate ability by identifying what you can ac-tually accomplish.

- *Responsibilities* or duties are passive. Duties just describe the details of the job description.

They are flat, boring, and assumed. *Accomplishments* are major successes you have had. Accomplishments are action-oriented statements that demonstrate a specific outcome that resulted from your actions or involvement. They are usually quantifiable or measurable.

We call resumes based on lists of duties "list resumes." They tend to be painfully boring. For example, everyone knows that sales people must sell a certain amount of widgets. However, unless you tell them, no one knows that you achieved 104% of your sales goal. A reader cannot ignore such a big accomplishment.

You need an action-oriented resume, not a list resume.

### Robert's Story

*A former co-worker, Robert, called after he was laid off. Did I have a copy of his job description so he could create a resume to find a new job?*

*No, I told him. You do not need a copy of your job description. You already know what you did all day. The better question is what did you accomplish? That is something very different. Robert's accomplishments make him different, more valuable than someone who just did a job description.*

Accomplishments make the reader curious about how you did your job, which separates you from the rest of the list resumes and the just plain awful resumes!

Here are some responsibilities picked from a real sales manager's resume:

- **Accountability to drive sales/margin plan in alignment with business goals**

*Comment:* Of course, a sales manager drives sales to achieve a specific goal. This statement does not really add anything.

- **Facilitate pricing decisions with oversight from Managers and Regional Managers**

*Comment:* Of course. Again, we all know that a sales manager facilitates pricing decisions. We all know that a sales manager might have a boss who gives oversight. So what?

- **Responsible for monthly turnover analysis**

*Comment:* So what? No one cares. What does this mean? In addition, this terminology is very specific to that company.

If we put careful thought into those experiences, it is possible to convert those duties into accomplishments that more fully describe the results you achieved in the past, results you could bring to a new company.

We can convert the statement, *"Accountability to drive sales/margin plan in alignment with business goals,"* into an action statement like this:

**Led team to achieve 123% of sales goal by increasing margin by two basis points by controlling inventory, labor costs, and increasing prices** *Comment:* By pulling out some actual results, the statement takes on an active voice. It makes the reader wonder, "How did he do that?" In this way, the statement attracts attention the way the other statement did not.

Let's convert *"Facilitate pricing decisions with oversight from Managers and Regional Managers"* into an active statement. By adding results, this ambiguous statement becomes impressive.

- **Implemented pricing program resulting in 3 basis point increase in margin by offering market pricing on commodity products and increasing pricing on specialty products**

**Comment:** The revised statement shows an active result – an accomplishment. It makes the reader ask, "How did she think of that?"

Again, we get an interesting, active statement when we change *"Responsibility for monthly turnover analysis"* to:

- **Reduced employee turnover by 20% by improving local management leadership skills**

*Comment:* The revision shows actual results making the reader curious to learn more.

This exercise of critically examining your accomplishments enables you to highlight the things can you do that will make you more interesting to potential employers. Your accomplishments give your brand substance.

### Sofia's Story

*Sofia taught college students how to teach science. So what? What image do you get of Sofia when you hear she taught college students how to teach science? I think it is pretty bland and flat. What is exciting or interesting about that?*

Does your impression of Sofia change if you learn that two of her students became teacher of the year in their first year of work? Or, that Sofia models active learning techniques to demonstrate effective active learning for science education? Pulling out the accomplishments shows the impact Sofia had on her students. She did more than just teach classes.

### Henry's Story

*Henry is a logistics consultant. His resume lists clients and assignments such as, "Reorganized distribution methods" and "Simplified movement of raw materials." So what? What was the impact of his consulting on his clients? What happened to those companies because he consulted about their logistics? How do those results relate to the position he wants next?*

Answering the "so what?" question is hard, much more difficult than making a list of responsibilities. However, including the answer to "so what?" makes you different. It makes you stand out among other candidates. It makes someone reading your resume ask themselves, "Gee, how did he do that?" This strategy helps employers view you as a viable candidate for their open positions.

**Now you try it!**

On the left side of a sheet of paper, write down the facts about your last job. Include everything you can think of.

On the right side of the paper, write down the accomplishments related to those facts. Include some statistics about how your actions made a difference.

**Exercise 4 –Your Accomplishments**

Highlight every responsibility in your worksheet. What impact did you provide to your company through that responsibility? Identify at least one or two accomplishments for each responsibility. Then go back to your current resume and start removing flat sounding accomplishments in favor of more active accom-plishments.

## Responsibilities vs. Accomplishments

**Responsibility 1** _____

Accomplishment 1 _____

Accomplishment 2 _____

**Responsibility 2** _____

Accomplishment 1 _____

Accomplishment 2 _____

**Responsibility 3** _____

Accomplishment 1 _____

Accomplishment 2 _____

**Responsibility 4** _____

Accomplishment 1 _____

Accomplishment 2 _____

**Responsibility 5** _____

Accomplishment 1 _____

Accomplishment 2 _____

Look at the differences between the two sets of statements. Which side is more interesting? What could someone learn about you from the information on the left side compared to the right side? Typically, the left side is a bland statement while the right side is more interesting and robust.

Although you need some facts in your resume, the results or accomplishments are more interesting and say more about you and your brand, about what you bring to the table, and who you are.

What do we mean by action words? What exactly is an action word? Consider including discussion of action words as those in Appendix 1. Consider the use of an active voice rather than a passive voice. For examples see Purdue's Writing Lab discussion at https://owl.english.purdue.edu/owl/resource/539/02/

It is possible to have too many accomplishments. You have space constraints. Your resume can only be one or two pages long, depending on your age and experience. Pick accomplishments that reflect well on you in your pursuit of a particular position. You do not want to include so much information about accomplishments that the reader feels he does not have to talk with you. Strive for a balance between too few and too many. Often the space considerations limiting paper resume to two pages helps achieve that balance.

## Exercise 5: Edit and Analyze

Consider each responsibility/accomplishment to determine if it relates to your desired job goal. Eliminate those that do not apply. In this exercise, we will examine each of your responsibility/accomplishment statements to determine the career goal it best describes. Label the career goal each of your responsibility/accomplishments best describes. You may find that some statements work well for many career goals while some are specific to only one.

## Key words

These days, computers often scan resumes for information, especially at larger companies. The computer programs are searching for specific key words supplied by the company reflecting qualities and experiences that they expect a qualified candidate to possess.

Your electronic resume must contain key words a company expects. Otherwise, your name will never make it through the first cut.

LinkedIn works the same way. Hiring managers use LinkedIn search tools to look for profiles that match the key words in positions they are trying to fill. If your LinkedIn profile does not contain those words, hiring managers will never find you.

What key words are right for you? You need to figure that out ahead of time. This takes a bit of research.

Job ads are a great place to find key words for positions that interest you. Hiring managers write job ads to describe precisely what they want in the right candidate. The job ads include the key words they are looking for. If you can find the right job descriptions through your research, you can identify the key words you should include in your resume to attract attention from hiring managers.

**Exercise 6: Key words**

This is a great way to identify the key words for your target job. Go back to the four or five dream jobs you found in Exercise 1. :

1. Read the job ads thoroughly. What words and phrases come up repeatedly in the description or the qualifications? Get beyond degree requirements. Pay particular attention to the skills and competency sections. Consider the behavior needed to do the job well, such as organized, detail oriented, communication skills. Also, consider the kind of work that will be done, such as LEAN, or vendor relations, or develop new markets. These are the key words the will appear consistently in ads for similar jobs.

2. You will include many of those words in your resume. You will come back to those key words when preparing to network and interview because those key words draw the correlation between your skills and the job requirements. When you include those key words, you appear to be qualified for the job you want!

*Tom's Story*

> *Tom is a process engineer with about 8 years of experience with one company since he graduated from college. He wants to change jobs and stay in his current geographic area. He wants to be sure his resume and other job search tools serve him well.*

The fix: looking at Tom's resume we found a list of responsibilities. The first step was to convert his responsibilities into accomplishments. Next, we needed to identify the right key words for his job goal. Armed with the proper language, we revised his accomplishment statements to include the appropriate key words. Reviewing the key words also prompted Tom to discover more accomplishments he had overlooked or discounted as unimportant.

First, we pulled up ads for Process Engineers on www.Indeed.com. We looked for four or five of these ads with good detailed descriptions of job duties.

Since Tom is not applying for any positions at this time, we only care about the detailed descriptions.

The ads follow a predictable format: a description of the company, the job responsibilities, and the position requirements. What words and phrases appear consistently in these advertisements?

As we read the ads for Process Engineers, we consistently see words like:

- Team, cross-functional team
- Process improvement, process documentation, process changes
- Cost reduction, quality improvements, capacity increases, cost savings
- Product development
- Technical solutions, emerging technologies
- Project plans, multiple projects
- Independent judgment
- Problem solving, troubleshoot, identify solutions
- Manufacturing environment
- Strong math and analytical skills
- Well organized, attention to detail, inquisitive
- Strong verbal and written skills, technical writing

Checking with Tom, he agreed these words reflected his experience as a Process Engineer. We adjusted

Tom's resume to describe his accomplishments using the key words found in the job ads.

When we are finished with the paper resume, Tom can update his LinkedIn profile to include the key words in the descriptions of the positions he has held and the Skills section. We will come back to the LinkedIn profile.

Since Tom's paper resume and virtual resume (LinkedIn profile) will be the same or very similar, including the right key words gave him advantages over other resumes:

- He passed the computer screens. Now a real person might actually read his resume
- His job search tools relate to what the companies are looking for so it puts him in their line of sight.
- Matching keywords made his LinkedIn profile searchable for companies and recruiters looking for people with his skills, reinforcing the use of the right key words.

## What not to include

Your resume is not the story of your life. It is a strategic tool to highlight the best parts of your background and place yourself in line of sight as you network. It is fine to leave off some things. You can have a sheet describing all the small details you might need on an employment application. However, that information does not go on your resume.

Here is a partial list of what *NOT* to include:

- *Months of employment.* Just include the years not the months. This keeps it simple, easy to read, and increases white space for a pleasing consistent look.
- *Salaries.* Never put salaries in writing, even if the employer asks for it. You want to share information with potential employers in conversations during interviews but you do not want to put it on a resume.
- *References.* References are valuable. You do not want to lose control over such important information by including names on a resume. It is also not necessary to say, "References available

upon request." Everyone knows that. Omit all reference from your resume.

- *Hobbies and Interests.* Leave them off unless your hobbies and interests are super special. Someone who has run 12 triathlons is different from someone who puts on their resume that they like to go to the gym. Running triathlons takes determination, skill, and energy, characteristics that most employers value. Going to the gym is not special. Leave it off.

- *Political or religious affiliations.* You cannot be certain that your political or religious affiliations are not going to offend someone so leave it off unless you are in a political or religious line of work.

- *Personal pronouns "I," "me," "we":* Most employers do not like the use of personal pronouns in resumes. However, the use of personal pronouns probably will not get your resume rejected. Writing your resume in the first person with personal pronouns is a little informal. Younger people often write resumes more informally with personal pronouns because it fits with a social media orientation. Most resumes, especially for professionals higher in an organization, are still written in the more formal third person voice, without personal pronouns. We advocate for third person without personal pronouns using phrases instead of full sentences because it makes the accomplishments stand out.

**Create Sizzle!**

Buzzwords: are they good or bad? Phrases like 'Team player,' 'Detailed-oriented,' 'Proven track record of success,' 'Go-to person,' 'Exceptional organizational skills' pop up in many resumes.

What do you think? Are they generally a good idea, or not?

We can evaluate whether they are a good idea by considering whether buzzwords get results. Are you confident that you will get a response because you included buzzwords in your resume? If not, then why continue to use buzzwords?

I have written or revised many resumes for people searching for a new job. I admit I occasionally use buzzwords. What is wrong with these buzz words —>'Excellent communication skills,' 'Leadership skills,' 'Go-to person,' 'Exceptional organizational skills,' or 'Self-starter?'

Buzzwords steal the sizzle from a resume, and drain it of its uniqueness. If you want your resume (virtual or paper) to make you stand out, consider using specifics instead.

**Specifics create sizzle.**

Let us compare buzz with sizzle:  The following e are examples of buzzwords that do little to inform or excite the reader. Look at how we can change that, making a much more interesting and informative presentation.

*Buzz:* 'Team player', 'excellent communication skills', 'problem solver', 'self-starter'

*Sizzle:* 'Six Sigma Green Belt', 'Persuasive presentations to increase sales', Lead cost reduction teams to improve quality', 'Marketing campaign to kick off new product'

When you move past the buzzwords, you get to more interesting accomplishments that describe your contributions better. That is what employers want to see.

Change that experience into some sizzle phrases. Identify clear and unique accomplishment-oriented experience, and the resume will sizzle and will be the friend you deserve in your job transition process.

## Modern day buzzwords

Every year you can find articles about buzzwords that have moved beyond useful and into tired. Tired buzzwords kill the sizzle. Some modern buzzwords have seen better days. Here is an example of a sentence in James' resume bogged down in buzzwords while failing to tell anything about the candidate, James.

*I delight in **exceeding customer expectations**, being a **team player** while being a **self-starter**, al-*

*ways driving initiatives to achieve bottom-line results.*

It is full of tired buzzwords that have lost their sizzle. Nothing in this sentence will attract a hiring manager's attention.

Let us break this buzzword sentence down to make it more effective. To do that we have to understand what James is trying to say. We have to ask some questions to get to the bottom of the story.

*Exceeding customer expectations:*

What actions result in exceeding customer expectations? How can we convert this outcome into a measurable statement? Let us examine at James' experience in more detail.

James says he exceeded expectations. What he does not say is he received an award for customer satisfaction. Rather than say he exceeding expectations, it would be much more powerful for James to talk about the recognition he received.

The revised phrase could be:

*Received President's Award for Excellent Customer Satisfaction*

OR

*Implemented Customer First campaign that increased customer satisfaction by 12% in first year.*

Notice that the result is more meaningful and makes more sense to a reader than saying James exceeded customer satisfaction.

*Team player:*

This is a good concept. How does "team player" manifest itself in James' life? James could describe an accomplishment that demonstrates that he is a team player. He could say:

Led productivity improvement team analyzing product rejections resulting in a 6% reduction in cost.

**OR**

Project leader for transition to new software platform, implemented without any business interruption.

Either of those action oriented phrases based on accomplishments demonstrate James' teamwork better than saying he is a "team player."

*Self-starter:*

What exactly does this mean anyway? The term is often used to mean "showing initiative" but it really has become a buzz word. Since James considers himself a self-started, he should consider providing an example of being a self-starter that demonstrates this characteristic better than the buzzword. On the other hand, he could select a better key word like "entrepreneurial approach." James could pair that descriptive phrase with a story about how he figured out a different way to handle customer complaints.

*Driving initiatives:*

What initiative are we talking about here? Instead of using the buzzword, James can describe a specific project or initiative he led. For example, James could say, "Identified $2 million in savings by changing paper vendor." Talking about an accomplishment is so much more descriptive and makes James stand out so much better from other candidates.

*Achieve bottom-line results:*

Of course you do! Everyone who survives in business achieves bottom line results most of the time. James could describe this better by referencing specific percentage increases. "Consistently exceeded annual sales quota" "Exceeded 105% of plan in five consecutive years".

**The bottom line:** Consider your accomplishments carefully so you can describe them in active manner balancing key words to make your point without using tired buzzwords.

## Omit the Obvious

With resume real estate at a premium, it is silly to waste valuable space on standard information that everyone expects.

Everyone expects sales people make cold calls and demonstrations to potential customers. It is part of the job. Likewise, everyone knows that architects read and write blue prints, IT people write code, and engineers perform tests. Your resume should describe what you accomplished not just the regular duties. How can we convert standard information into something that makes a candidate look more interesting?

*If you are a sales person:*

Describe sales results compared to quota, a particularly large or complicated sale you are proud of, or sales growth over prior year in a new territory.

- Exceeded sales quota by 23% for six consecutive years.
- Established new territory increasing annual sales by 36%

*If you are in information technology:*

Describe the amount of new business the new system brought in or how you completed the project on time and under budget.

- Implemented Field Change notice system resulting in 45% decrease in redundant maintenance activities.

- Designed systems to streamline order processing resulting in 25% reduction in delivery delays with 15% decrease in product returns.

*If you are an engineer:*

Describe improvements made or new process innovations. Consider highlighting examples such as,

- Designed and obtained patent for Widget for sheet fed printing systems.
- Developed modifications to old products and development of new products based on field observations resulting in 5% reduction in raw material cost.

Include the information that makes you different or makes you particularly successful in your role.

## Exercise 6: Eliminate the Expected

Review each of your accomplishments and edit out the expected information that just takes up space. Replace it with examples of your own personal achievements to make yourself stand out.

# Chapter 5

# Organizing Your Story

### Simple and consistent is best

You want your resume to be the best reflection of who you are since it speaks for you when you are not present. It should be simple, clear, and consistent, even if you are not. A simple resume is best because it is easiest to read.

The best resumes are consistent in their layout and formatting. A clear consistent structure ensures that the information stands out. Do not distract readers with messy layouts and distracting text.

**Lay Out**

Layout is important. Recruiters spending hours reading resumes want to see information in a familiar way. Having a layout consistent with what recruiters recognize makes their lives easier. That means that your information is more likely to read and understand.

*Your Name:* Capitalized your name in a simple bold font of at least 16-points. Your name should be the most noticeable thing on your resume. The larger font draws attention to the owner. What kind of confidence does the name in tiny font suggest? Be proud of who you are and place your name in a clear and prominent spot on the page. Arial Black is an excellent font choice for your name because it stands out well. Make your name easy to identify by placing it centered on the top line. You may also try aligning it to the left as an alternative. Other "fancy" or "interesting" alternatives just tend to distract, not draw attention to you.

*Contact Information:* Second in importance to who you are is how to contact you. Place your contact information tight across the top directly under your name. You need to include your phone number and email address.

Your email address can say a lot about you. Make sure the message it sends is of an important and serious professional. If your email address is a funny one or something that means something special to you, like "chicken35," "cuddlynana," or "bigpartygirl," you need to consider if this is the image you want your prospective employer to have of you. It might be time to get a new email address.

Gmail accounts are the ubiquitous standard for email service. They are easy to get and make you appear technologically savvy. The best kind of address is the one that has your name in the address. That way, your address reinforces your name with your contact. It is assuring and professional.

You do not need to label your contact information. Everyone can tell the difference between an email address and a phone number. If you are including multiple phone numbers, do distinguish which is "Home," "Fax," or "Cell."

*Headline or Objective:* Select a short phrase describing the job you want. Put it across the top, in bold capital letters right under your contact information. Do not write a paragraph. Write a few words that capture the qualifications highlighted in your resume. If you are looking for a human resource leadership position then say "HUMAN RESOURCE EXECUTIVE." If you were looking for a process engineering position then you would say "PROCESS ENGINEER." This tells everyone exactly what you want.

*Key words:* Short phrases listed at the top of your resume that describe what you have done and what identifies your expertise. These words will come from the Responsibilities you identified in Exercise 3. Create a two columns table to help keep the formatting even and make it is easier to read. Consider using bullets to make the key words stand out.

*Headings:* Most people separate sections with bold capitalized labels like, "PROFESSIONAL EXPERIENCE," "EDUCATION AND TRAINING." Headings make for a pleasing layout. Keep headings simple and related to the section. We prefer that headings be bold and capitalized.

*Bullets:* Make important points stand out and easier to read by targeting the information with bullets. Use a simple and consistent in shape and size. Avoid wingdings like bats and hearts, which can distract the reader away from what you have to offer. Remember, we want people to read the information, not distract them with fancy gimmicks.

Prioritize your information using an outline style structure. Major headings should align with the left margin. Supporting information should indent incrementally below the headings. Be sure your outline scheme is consistent throughout the resume.

*Consistent Fonts:* Pick one font and stick with it. Acceptable fonts include Times New Roman, Ariel, and Calibri. These fonts translate well when transmitted electronically and are generally easy to read. Avoid underlining and symbols because they distract and get messy. Select a font size that looks good for the information you are providing. Generally, a font of 10 to 12 will be easiest to read and still let you get your information on the limited number of pages available. Always use a black font. Colors are distracting and draw attention away from your uniform appearance.

*Bold, Capitalize and Italics:* Use bold and italics to make important points stand out. A good strategy is to put company or school names in bold capital letters.

*Locate Information Consistently:* Align all company names on the left margin and align dates with on the left margin. List company names and dates on one line with your job title beneath it, aligned on the left.

*Two Page Limit:* If it is longer than two pages, start editing.

*Contact information on page two:* What happens if the second page of your two-page resume becomes separated from the first page with the contact information? How will anyone ever find you? Make sure you put your name and email address or telephone number on

the top page 2. Place it in the header. Align your name
to the left with an indication that this is page 2 and
your contact aligned on the right. It should look something like this,

| Katherine Burik, Page 2 | Katherine @ InterviewDoc.com |
|---|---|

*Maximize Real Estate:* Put the most important information on the top half of the first page where readers
can find it easily. Readers are less likely to read information at the bottom or on the second page of a resume. They might look quickly at degree information
or certifications but the more recent and most important information should be on the top half of the
first page.

*Education Information: The Ladders* study reported that
recruiters are likely to look to the bottom or back of a
resume to look for a college degree if it is required for
the position. They are likely to note the school name
and degree type but do not usually spend much time
reading details. If you are a job seeker with work expe-

rience, put your education at the end, following experience. Recent college graduates, lacking much relevant experience, should generally put education on the first page right under the objective, since it is your most important credential until you develop on the job experience. Once you have acquired some work experience, your work competencies become more important than the degree.

If you graduated more than 10 years ago, leave off the years. For older job seekers, including the graduation dates indicates your age. There is no need to draw attention to that. The experience is what has value, focus on that.

Layout for education could look something like this. If you need to conserve space, it could all fit on one line.

**Northwestern University,** Evanston, IL  BA History, Graduated with honors

*White Space:* This refers to the amount of space on the page that is unmarked. White space gives a reader pauses or breaks and provides an opportunity for eyes to rest. White space also provides a place for people to write comments or make notes. It is important to find a balance between text and white space. Your resume should have a pleasing look to it. It should not look like you tried to smash too many words on to a single page. Use Print Preview or print a hard copy of your resume and hold it out in front of you. Does it look messy? Does it look crowded? Is it overly dark, with too much writing? Are the margins appropriate on the top, bottom, and sides so the content does not look crowded in the center or as if it is running off the page? If not, begin adjusting the space between paragraphs and the margin size until you find a pleasing balance. Be sure that the spacing between paragraphs is consistent throughout.

*Symbols:* Symbols do not always translate electronically so avoid symbols if possible.

## Using Key Words Strategically

Key words show up repeatedly on a paper resume and in a LinkedIn profile. In a paper resume, key words appear in the special key word table at the top of the resume and appear in the body of the resume as you describe the accomplishments associated with each job. Be sure to use the same words or phrases in your description of accomplishments as you used in your table. This consistent use of phrases provides consistency and reinforces your abilities.

Tom, the process engineer, found key words like these in his research of the kinds of positions he was looking for:

- Team, cross-functional team
- Process improvement, process documentation, process changes
- Cost reduction, quality improvements, capacity increases, cost savings
- Product development
- Technical solutions, emerging technologies
- Project plans, multiple projects
- Independent judgment
- Problem solving, troubleshoot, identify solutions
- Manufacturing environment
- Strong math and analytical skills
- Well organized, attention to detail, inquisitive

- Strong verbal and written skills, technical writing

Tom's table of key words might look something like this, assuming Tom has typical process engineer experiences:

- Technical solutions to solve problems in a manufacturing environment

- Cost reduction and process improvements to reduce cost and improve quality

- Cross-functional team leadership

- Well organized project management

- Strong math and analytic skills

- Strong communication skills, technical writing

In your paper resume, insert a two-column table immediately below your objective title. Use this space to list your principle skills and abilities – the ones you identified in the earlier exercise and are highlighting in the rest of the resume. Let the language speak for itself by removing borders and omitting shading. The remaining table looks clean and focuses attention on that information.

This table is not a substitute for solid descriptions of accomplishments in the body of your resume. However, it does serve to highlight special key words or qualifications so they are not lost in the body or the back. This makes it easier for the reader to identify what you bring to the table.

## Printing and Paper

Occasionally you will need to print your resume to carry with you to a meeting. This is an important opportunity to make an impression. Use good quality white paper such as 24 pound paper with a high brightness count such as 96 or higher. This makes the resume seem substantial. The Brightness factor makes the black print stand out. Do not use colored or bright papers. Let the resume speak for itself.

Be careful to match the paper to the printer you are using. Laser and inkjet printers use different kinds of ink. Laser paper tends to have a coating to enable the ink to sit on top while inkjet paper is generally rougher so the ink can soak into the paper. Documents printed from inkjet printers onto laser paper tend to smear.

Similarly, documents printed from laser printers onto inkjet paper tend to be a bit blurry. Invest a little in the quality of paper so your resume looks great and leaves a great impression.

**Use Relevant Credentials**

Since our goal is to focus on the specific abilities you bring to your dream job, not everything you have ever done will be included in your resume. Only include the credentials related to the job you seek.

For example, let us say you started your career in teaching but switched to engineering because it was more your passion. Unless your teaching credentials relate to your new engineering career, leave them off, especially if you need to conserve space. You want potential employers to see you as an engineer. Your teaching career was great but that is not who you are now. Only include the credentials that define who you are now and what you want potential employers to see.

# Chapter 6

## Problems with Resumes

If you made it this far, you have put a great deal of effort into building the perfect resume. Despite all that work, simple mistakes can seriously detract from the brand image you are trying to create. We can learn a lot about good resumes by looking at some classic bad one.

In a dark locked drawer in a black file cabinet in my basement, I keep a collection of the worst resumes in the world. This is where bad resumes go to die. These bad resumes have a dark personality that reflects a cluttered mind. They remind us of tired old vegetables – week-old soft carrots with dried spots and limp greens. They look like the owners desperate attempt to send something – anything – to meet a request or fill a need. That is not the impression you are trying to send.

Some bad resumes simply look looks. It may be a poor copy of a facsimile with a coffee stain on the corner. Sometimes it comes on colored paper. It might have three or four different fonts. Maybe it is a confusion of many different font sizes. It might include odd formatting that obscures the flow of information.

We can make sure we make the best impression by looking at those bad resumes and using those mistakes as guides to fix our own.

**Worst Resume in the World**

There is surprisingly stiff completion for the title of Worst Resume. Like most HR people with years of experience recruiting employees, I have seen many bad resumes. Here are some outstanding Worsts.

*The three-page resume on bright red paper.* That was a doozy. This fellow came to an interview for internal promotion with a three-page resume printed on bright red paper. He joined the company only five years earlier so he had a successful job search resume in the recent past. He should have known better. He was a talented fellow with good results in his current job. He was well qualified for the promotion. However, if all I knew about him were the bright red resume, I would never have talked to him in a million years.

*The six-page resume.* This very talented fellow totally hid his exceptional experience in a mountain of superfluous information. It buried all his excellent achievements. I made it to page three before putting it aside.

*The resume with five different fonts of different size and mismatched formatting.* This resume meandered all over the place with text that jumped in size and varied between italics, bold and plain fonts. It was confusing, annoying, and distracting.

*The one with way too many words.* The author of this resume must have thought that if he kept talking he would eventually say the right thing. Not so. I could not figure out what he wanted, where he worked, or what kinds of jobs he held. He buried the important information under mountains of text. Nothing stood out.

*The resume from a party girl.* Bigpartygirl @ hot-pants.com unfortunately included her Facebook link with her email address. The pictures on her social media page indicated she was indeed a big party girl. It was difficult to take her serious. The party girl image reflected by her email address and Facebook postings ruled her out of consideration.

Do not overwhelm your brand with unintended messages. Search out any negative messages that may take away from the professional brand you want to represent.

## What's the Deal with Tipos Anyway?

Huh? There is something wrong with that title sentence… Where is my spell check…? That's write. It is a typo not a tipo. No one will notice, write?

Actually, people notice and care whether you spell words correctly, use the proper tense, select the correct word for the context, or use the right punctuation.

When I see a typographical error, I want to pull out my red pen and let the world know.

Typographical errors are an outward sign of a careless mind. Typos suggest that you do not pay attention to details or that you are illiterate, whether that is true or not. Sometimes it sends the message that you do not think much of yourself or what you offer since you did not take the time to make sure your work was correct. It is hard enough to connect with your next employer without tripping over your own words.

I have known hiring managers who refused to consider even the most qualified candidate if he or she had a typo in his/her resume or cover letter. One vice president I worked with always specifically asked whether the candidate I referred to him had any typos in the resume or cover letter. Even a stray punctuation mark disqualified an otherwise great candidate.

I know of one recruiter who actually got out the red pen to edit the offending resume and sent the marked document back to its owner. That candidate was eliminated from consideration. Resumes with typos and incorrect word choices happen more often than you would expect and often make it into the HR team's special private "Hall of Shame" collection.

Some of these mistakes can be funny. Here are a few:

"I am great with the pubic."

"Am a perfectionist and rarely if if ever forget details."

"Received a plague for Salesperson of the Year."

"I'm intrested to here more about that."

"I'm working today in a furniture factory as a drawer."

Other HR people have their favorites too. These are some examples from a recent SHRM survey:

"I am about to enrol on a Business and Finance Degree with the Open University. I feel that this qualification will prove detrimental to me for future success."

"Seeking a party-time position with potential for advancement."

It is not hard laugh at these gems. These examples came from real resumes submitted by real, well-meaning folks trying hard to land their next jobs. It is serious business. How big of an impact do these kinds of mistakes have?

According to a SHRM survey of HR Managers in 2005, 87% of respondents would not consider candidates with a resume or cover letter with grammatical errors or typos. That is a very strong message. Check, double check, and spell check to make sure you are saying what you mean to say. Ask someone else to read what you have written. Often you overlook these kinds of mistakes because you know what you are trying to say. Unbiased eyes are better able to spot errors.

## Top 5 Problems with Resumes

Awful resumes have some common elements. Since we often learn more from mistakes than successes, here are the top five problems with awful resumes.

### 1. Ugly, hard to read

There is nothing as distracting as a poorly laid out, hard to read resume, especially a resume with paragraph after paragraph of words in small print without a lot of visible space. If it is hard to read and I have an option to read someone else's resume, then I will put your resume aside.

*The fix:* Read your resume carefully. Print it out and read it again. Use good quality white paper and a very good printer. Stand back from the page and look at the lay out. If the printed resume looks off balance or has too many words on the page then go back to edit. Be brutal. Only include the information that supports your claim that you should have the job you want.

## 2. No objective

Remember, the employer will not take the time to figure out, from the contents of your resume, exactly what kind of position you are looking for. Unless you say what you want, how can anyone help you? Your resume will be put aside. Sometimes when people get desperate, they will say, "I'll do anything." However, the reality is you have a preference and you are good at something.

*The fix:* Say what you want. Put your preference in the very top so the person reading your resume knows what you want. The answer will be either yes or no. However, if you do not say what you want the answer will always be no. Take a stand.

### 3. Lack of Focus

Related to the resumes that do not say what you want, this kind of resume is an unremarkable list of jobs and responsibilities with nothing to distinguish your resume from the next one.

You do not know how many people are applying for the position you want. How will you distinguish yourself from those other candidates? Recruiters will want to talk to the person who can show they are talented, special, and bring something special to the table.

*The fix:* Your accomplishments differentiate you from the next person. Tell the reader how satisfied your customers were with your service. Describe your sales results. Make sure the recruiter knows you did more than answer the phone. Be specific and be proud.

### 4.   Too long, babbling

I recently saw a five-page resume with paragraph after paragraph of information that I did not want to know. I put it aside and rubbed my eyes. Everyone else reading that resume will put it aside too.

*The fix:* Keep it short and to the point. Limit yourself to no more than two pages. People early in their career need only one page. Make every word count. Edit, edit, edit.

### 5.   Not relevant to the position you seek

Clearly, if you are building a resume you want a job. However, sending your resume to every job opening listed on Indeed.com does not improve your chances. It takes up time and results in more rejections. That will not get you any closer to your goal.

*The fix:* Design your resume to be a strategic reflection of who you are and what you want, and why you should have it. People will notice. You will get positive attention for the positions you want and for which you are qualified. Honest. It really works.

## How long is too long?

Best practice rules of thumb tell us that resumes are either one or two pages long. Young people early in their careers usually have one page resumes. More experienced people have more to share so they can have two page resumes.

This simple answer rather misses the point. Every word must serve a purpose. Use the fewest possible words to make your point. If you can convey your message in one page, then even an experienced person can have a one-page resume.

I created a two-page resume for Laura, a controller with about 30 years of experience. It looked great and did everything she wanted it to do. One day she responded to a job posting that requested each applicant submit a one-page resume. I took the challenge and discovered that taking a red pen to an already nice resume made a great one-page resume. The shorter resume came directly to the point and put a sharp point on her abilities. As a result, it directly targeted the position she wanted.

### Elyse's Story

*Elyse is 24, only two years out of college. She specializes in political campaigns. She started working on campaigns in college. She has worked on five campaigns in progressively more responsible roles.*

In Elyse's line of work, many people have had five jobs in three years. She already needs a two-page resume now despite her young age because she must demonstrate the increase in responsibility.

Here are some guidelines when considering length.

- If your resume is one page with a little bit on the second page, start editing to make it one page. No one will look at the second page.
- If your resume is a full two pages and you are in your twenties or thirties, it is probably too long. Start editing.
- If your resume is uses paragraphs to describe things or has narrow margins, whether it is one or two pages, start editing.

- If your resume is more than two pages, regardless of your age or experience, start editing.

Prioritize, itemize, and be specific. Make the most of the space you have available.

# Posting your Resume on LinkedIn

LinkedIn is the largest professional database in the world. Recruiters and companies use LinkedIn to find candidates. Every job seeker needs a LinkedIn profile that reflects the same information you have in your paper resume.

LinkedIn's structure allows you to organize your profile to highlight your special qualifications. There is a special, searchable section for key words. Use this section to include the important key words you identified in the resume building process.

If you do not already have a LinkedIn profile, create one today. It is easy. Use the Edit feature to add or change the information for your profile.

*Headline*: This is your objective – the short phrase that describes or identifies the job you want.

*Location and Industry:* Enter the country and postal code of your preferred location. LinkedIn will provide options for Location Name. Select the one you prefer.

Industry is trickier. This is a pull down menu with limited choices. Select the option that most closely reflects the industry you want to work in. Sometimes Industry means reflects a profession like "Marketing and Advertising" and sometimes it reflects an actual industry like "Oil and Energy." Find the one that best matches your goals.

*Contact Information:* Complete this section with your professional email address. Your phone number and address are optional.

You can also add your Twitter address and any websites where you display your skills. If you have a special slideshow or graphic resume, insert it here so your LinkedIn profile describes all aspects of your skills and abilities.

*Summary:* LinkedIn allows you to describe yourself in more casual terms than a formal paper resume. For the Summary section, use the keywords from your resume to create a conversational narrative about you. Do not be afraid to use the word "I." Try writing this section in a separate document where you have access to spell check and other editing features. Then transfer the completed summary to LinkedIn.

You can upload videos or slide shows that help you tell your story. Dan and I have videos of us talking about our approach to answering some important interviewing questions and a Prezi file describing our first book. We update our profiles regularly to keep information current and interesting.

*Experience: Complete this section by copying the information from your paper resume.* You will need the following information for each position:

- Company Name
- Title
- Location
- Time Period

- Description

Use the "Description" box, to post the text and formatting from your paper resume and paste in this box. If you prefer, you can edit the text to make it a more of a narrative or use the space to explain a particularly important point in more detail than you might have in the paper resume.

You can use the arrows on the right side of each entry to reposition the location of the information. The most recent information goes at the top, the oldest at the end.

*Skills & Expertise:* These are key words too. You can add up to 52 words and phrases that represent your skills and expertise, far more than you have space for on your paper resume. Take advantage of all 52 words. By including as many searchable key words as you can, recruiters can find you more easily. Include every variations of the term you identified in Exercise 1.

We suggest you pick words related to three aspects of who you are:

1. Professional skills related to the kind of work you do

2. The industry you are in or want to work in

3. Your personal skills and strengths, like leadership, teamwork, organizational, conflict resolution

Once entered, these skills and expertise words will be visible when your profile is finished. Periodically, LinkedIn will ask your connections to "endorse" you, a way others have of indicating their confidence in any of those abilities. Over time, these endorsements begin to reflect what the members of your professional community thinks of your abilities. This is way to strengthen your brand. The Skills and Expertise section changes as people start to express their perspective of their interactions with you.

Some people think this is silly. I disagree. When I reach out to connect with someone, it is the first section I look at. This section is almost as important as recommendations or references because your contacts are giving an opinion about what you do well. If you begin endorsing other people, they will endorse you. This is a good thing.

*Education:* Unlike your paper resume, you can include all your education on LinkedIn. Because you can never be sure where your next contact will come from, it is often a good idea to include the high school you attended. The education feature lets you access all the people who attended that school. That is a whole group of people you might not otherwise be able to access. Be sure to include clubs, sororities/fraternities, and service organizations you belonged to in school as well. These provide additional connections you might find useful.

*Additional Information:* LinkedIn offers you the chance to add personal information that you would not include in your paper resume. Go ahead. It makes you appear well rounded and gives potential contacts ways to connect with you. You can add your interests in gardening, running, and boating if you want.

*Organizations:* Add the organizations to which you belong. Keep it professional. It is not necessary to add your fantasy football league, although it may not hurt.

### Reviewing Your Profile

You make your LinkedIn profile a strategic job search tool by doing these things:

- Inserting key words to describe yourself in these places:
  - o The summary under your name
  - o In the Background section Summary
  - o In the description of each position

- Having a robust summary and headline that attracts attention and makes a positive statement about what you offer

- Utilizing all 52 strategic key words in the Skills and Expertise section

- Adding slide shows, PowerPoint presentations, articles you wrote, and other business related materials that demonstrate your skills

- Connecting other websites and social media accounts that demonstrate what you can do

- Expanding your contacts and Groups to connect with people who can advance your job search

# Chapter 8

## Special Circumstances

### Resumes for young people

We often hear from young candidates that they cannot get the job they want because it requires experience. Sometimes college students have more experience than they think they have.

### Terrence's Experience

*Terrence is graduating from Ohio State University with an engineering degree specializing in medical technology design. He has two summer internships with some real accomplishments. However, he expected his first job would be entry level. Why? He has significant experience. Why downgrade his ex-*

*perience just because he is young? What kind of story should he tell?*

Terrence's resume should treat his internships and research as regular jobs. He should identify and highlight those accomplishments in detail. He has more accomplishments than do many engineers with more years. He should be confident and demonstrate that his experience makes him more than an entry-level person. He needs a resume for an experienced worker.

What are the significant accomplishments you obtained in classes or activities during school? Consider summer work and internships. These accomplishments are valuable work experience. These accomplishments go into your resume.

Current students should deliberately select college experiences that support future job search. If you are still in school, sign up for internships and take jobs in college that show you are responsible. Consider service roles that also provide the opportunity to show initiative.

Here are some tips for resumes for younger people:

*Resumes are usually one page.* Younger people have less experience and therefore require less space to highlight accomplishments and establish your brand. There are exceptions but this is the general rule of thumb.

*Education in the top third of the first page.* This is your most important accomplishment so it should be front and center.

*Identify every accomplishment.* Even if you delivered pizza, you contributed to the business's success. What special contribution did you make? Think carefully. Did you help train other workers, you come in early to make the dough every day, or did you identify a new way to market. Each of these is important. Look for details.

## Resumes for older people

Older people have the opposite problem. They have so many accomplishments and perhaps so many jobs that it is difficult to create a resume that focuses on the most important elements or reveals the brand. Experienced workers must identify their goal then edit furiously to cut away all extemporaneous information that does not support their goal.

Here are some tips for resumes for older people:

*Education goes on the back page* without much detail unless the detail is special. Keep Phi Beta Kappa, graduating with honors, or Rhodes Scholar. Omit the GPA. Be sure to include your major and perhaps a minor, especially if it relates to your job objective.

*Take dates off education.* It only puts attention on your age.

*Two pages are probably required.* Be sure your most recent jobs are on page one.

*Page 2 is less important.* Use less description on page two.

*Use a list for older positions early in your career.* It takes up less space and does not distract from your brand, the information you want people to see.

*Consider leaving very early positions off your resume,* especially if you changed careers. Those early positions do not necessarily add to your credentials.

## Funny Sounding Names

We worked with a candidate who had received his university's award as the top in his field. He won awards from the professional organization in his field and had excellent references. Every year the winners of these awards are the first ones hired. However, by the end of the summer after graduation, he still did not have a job. His professor sent us his resume. Maybe that was the problem.

I took one look at it and identified the problem right away. His name was Etoli Yvnaaki. Although it is a great name and belongs to a great person with a great story, the name is also very intimidating. Hiring managers who saw his resume had how to address this person. Is it a man or a woman? How would do you address someone if you do not know whether it is a man or a woman or how to pronounce the name? How could they call him on the phone to ask for more information? What would they say?

I suggested adding a nickname to clarify his gender and provide clues to pronounce his name correctly. We changed the name on his resume to this:

**ETOLI (ETHAN) YVNAAKI**

He sent his resume out again to his target schools and immediately the calls poured in. Within two weeks, he had three job offers.

The difference was in providing his name in accessible terms hiring managers could understand. The hiring managers were not biased; they just did not want to look stupid or offend the candidate. Providing clues that help the hiring manager a little will come back to help you in the end.

Etoli never had to use the nickname Ethan. Once he was able to talk to people, he could teach them to pronoun his name. However, until he could start those conversations, he needed to remove this barrier from his job search so he could get what he wanted.

## Holes in Time

Hiring managers do not like holes in time, those disturbing gaps of unemployment in your record.

### Joe's Story

> Joe has a decent record of accomplishment as a financial
> analyst, working for several large companies in his town.
> That is except for the eight-month period of unemployment in between his last job and the one before that. He
> finds that hole in time to be embarrassing but he is not
> sure how to avoid talking about it or putting it on his resume. He feels it stands out like a sore thumb.

**The Fix:** Joe may have an excellent explanation for why he took eight months to find a job but until he gets to speak to someone, the explanation does not matter. We do not lie or exaggerate but we can tell the story that makes us look best.

Sometimes the best way to make a hole in time disappear is to use years instead of months in the dates of employment. This is not lying or exaggerating but it can be a good way to minimize a potentially damaging subject.

Joe was laid off in September 2005 and found his next position in May 2006. We can hide the hole by using years without months. Joe can show one position ending in 2005 and the other position beginning in 2006.

## Returning to Work

When returning to the workforce after raising children, you must not only explain that significant hole in time on your resume, you must also demonstrate that you still have relevant skills. This requires advanced planning.

*Penelope's Story*

> *Penelope was a mid-level IT manager when she had her second child at 30 years of age. She and her husband decided she would stay home with the children until the youngest started kindergarten. She was active in PTA, putting her project management skills to work running the annual bazaar. She continued to attend her professional association and became a board member responsible for programs.*

*When it was time to return to work she continued to use her last resume but got no action. She was not sure how to restructure her resume to make her previous experience relevant to her job search today.*

It is easiest to retain your skills if you kept active in your field while you stayed at home by staying active in your professional or industrial association, taking classes, or doing some consulting work. This is especially true in technical fields like IT.

If your resume stops when you left the workforce to raise children, hiring managers might wonder if you still have the skills, knowledge, and stamina necessary to pick up where you left off in your previous career. Hiring managers want to bring someone into the team that slides right in without effort. They do not want to retrain you.

Penelope needs to structure her resume to demonstrate that she can easily fit into the current team. She can highlight her project management work with the PTA and describe the way she stayed active with her professional association board.

If you are returning to work after a break in service, you can demonstrate your continued relevance in some of the following ways:

*Volunteer work: Participate* at your children's school or local charities. Use these experiences to practice and sharpen your professional skills.

*Consulting work: You do not* necessarily need to have consistent, full-time employment to stay current. Consider providing your services as a consultant on small or short-term jobs.

*LinkedIn.* Get active in LinkedIn prior to starting your job search. Accumulate contacts and create a profile. Join relevant groups and start making comments and contributing ideas to get your brand known in advance of starting your job search. Holes in your resume will be less important when you have a credible presence with others in your field.

**Resumes for Levels of Experience**

Resumes serve different purposes depending on the level of employment. Therefore, the resume for an executive might look different from a resume for the resume for an entry-level position.

*Executives*

Executives are much more likely to get a position through networking so a resume is more of a reference tool. What you say to the people you meet is much more important than the actual resume. Paper and virtual resumes for executives must support the accomplishments that the executive talks about in stories. Executive resumes focus on accomplishments in bullet points using minimum words. The table with key words and competencies is especially important.

Hiring managers often select executives based on how their personality and practices "fit" the organization. Your resume should include key words about your leadership style and approach.

## *Professionals and middle managers*

Professionals and middle managers should have a robust LinkedIn profile to assist with networking through LinkedIn. Your profile should be at 100% complete so people looking for someone with your talent can find you. Highlight leadership skills and project management experiences that demonstrate you can manager business objectives to successful completion.

## *Entry Level Individuals*

Entry-level resumes should be simple, easy to read, and brief. Provide a direct link between your experience and the job you want. Entry-level job seekers are just beginning to build their career. They need to be able to demonstrate how their abilities and experience apply to their new field.

## Functional vs. Chronological Resumes

Most resumes are chronological, starting with the most recent job and moving back in time until the first job. This works for most people. It is easiest to read and is the resume format most hiring managers and recruiters expect.

Chronological resumes have a standard format from top to bottom including:

- Name and contact information
- Objective shown in a phrase (headline) under contact information
- Key words in a table
- Professional experience with positions listed in reverse chronological order starting from the most recent
- Education at the bottom for experienced people or at the top for those recently out of college
- Credentials

Functional resumes are structured around the accomplishments for specific skills you wish to highlight. The order is a little different from top to bottom:

- Name and contact information
- Objective shown in a phrase under contact information
- Key words in a table are optional since a functional resume will have key words throughout

- Instead of positions listed in reverse chronological order starting from the most recent, substitute the major competencies for the job you seek
- Education is still at the bottom for experienced people or at the top for those recently out of college
- Credentials

A resume for a position as an HR Executive would list the general functions for an HR Executive and insert accomplishments from any position held that supports the qualifications for this position. It might look something like this:

*Training and Development*
- Accomplishment1 (from any job held)
- Accomplishment 2 (from any job held)

*Employee Relations*
- Accomplishment1 (from any job held)
- Accomplishment 2 (from any job held)

*Compensation and Benefits*
- Accomplishment1 (from any job held)
- Accomplishment 2 (from any job held)

At the end of a functional resume is usually a list of the positions held in chronological order from most recent to earliest with dates but without the explanation and accomplishments found in a chronological resume.

A functional resume provides an alternative way to share your experiences. Some recruiters think a functional resume is a way to hide something, as if the candidate is hiding substance with fluff and prose while lacking real information to support the candidate's abilities. We often see functional resumes for people changing careers, people with a hole in their experience, or people who got bad advice. We seldom recommend functional resumes since recruiters and hiring managers do not like reading them.

Bottom line: Use the resume that best displays your talents and gets attention. Unless you have some specific reason to use one, it is probably best to skip the functional resume. Stick with the format that corresponds to hiring managers' needs and displays information in the way they expect to see it.

## Unconventional resumes

We have focused on how to build a traditional resume that highlights your strengths in a way that employers understand and meets their needs. Although that is the norm, we have seen some beautiful unconventional resumes, mostly for creative types. Graphics designers, advertising, web designers, artists, and other creative people sometimes want a resume that demonstrates what they can do graphically rather than with words in a standard format.

If you want an unconventional resume in addition to a standard resume, you have several options.

*Your own website.* This is a great place to put work samples. You can direct people to your website through LinkedIn, tying together standard and unconventional methods of highlighting your talent.

*A Presume:* This is a software or online tool for the graphical representation of your employment information. Often such software enables you to create slide-show software, with your own voice for a soundtrack, describing your personal and work history and presenting your pitch.

*SlideRocket:* This presentation software can be used to create a graphic representation of your experiences.

*Prezi:* An alternative to PowerPoint, a Prezi combines video, slides, and sound in unlimited possibilities to create a display your skills in a unique way (Jackman, 2012).

Your graphic resume can contain pie charts, word maps, and photos or any combination you think best displays your unique talents. This is not a substitute for a well-written conventional resume but it is a great, creative addition to communicate your story. You can send these unconventional resume to people via social media as a way to start the conversation and get some attention.

# Chapter 9

## The Value of Consistency

Make your search tools consistent so your resume reflects the same story as your LinkedIn profile and what you say when you network and interview.

A resume is only one tool among many you will use to get a new position. Your job search needs a consistent strategy that reflects your brand in all the places potential employers will learn about you. Your search tools must be consistent across all those tools, supported by a well thought out Job Search Marketing Plan so you know where you are going and what you want to do.

What does that really mean? Recruiters value simplicity. They want to find candidates that meet their needs. You want to put yourself square in their view with a simple, consistent approach.

Let us consider Henry, the logistics manager. He structures his Job Search Marketing Plan with these tools to support his strategic goal:

- A solid understanding of what he wants and why he should have it
- A resume highlighting his goals and accomplishments with ties to key words for the position he seeks
- Business cards using the same font, contact information, and goal as his resume and LinkedIn profile address
- A LinkedIn profile highlighting the same goals and accomplishments as his resume with ties to key words for the position he seeks
- Contacts in LinkedIn, Facebook, and in his address book
- His email address will be consistent in his resume, LinkedIn profile, business cards, and in all correspondence with any contacts in any of his databases

Tight consistency in your job search tools will support your Personal Job Search Marketing Plan by making you look like you know what you are doing. You look organized and competent. You are easy to find because you are more searchable for positions you seek. You can more easily find contacts related to your search objective.

## Now What?

Your resume is perfect. Your LinkedIn account is 100% complete. Now what?

Focus on your Personal Job Search Marketing Plan. Network to find people who can help you at the companies where you want to work. Meet more people. Keep talking until you find the right person. Get business cards made and hand them out. Talk about yourself and highlight the information on your resume.

Prepare for interviews by selecting the particular stories from your experience that best support your goals. Check out "Tell Me About Yourself…," the third book in the Job Seeker Manifesto, to make the best impression during interviews.

134

## Sample Resume – Page One

---

# YOUR NAME

000 Street Avenue      Chicago, IL 60600                    (000) 000-0000          YName@gmail.com

## YOUR CAREER GOAL HEADLINE

- Server and desktop virtualization
- Envision creative, efficient infrastructure solutions from big systems to details
- Excellent written and oral communication
- Strong problem solving and troubleshooting abilities

- Master new technology and skills rapidly
- Wireless networking, security, and multiple operating systems and network protocols
- Manage projects and teams effectively
- Excellent leadership skills

### EXPERIENCE

**MOST RECENT COMPANY**  Dallas TX                                         2006 to Present
*Title*
Responsible for capacity planning for IT infrastructure and 550 user community including maintenance, troubleshooting, repair and system optimization. Administered Blackbaud accounting and school-management systems.

➢ Innovation
- Accomplishment related to innovation that could take a line or two to write using as few words as possible to get the most emphasis on the what you did
- Accomplishment related to something else that you did that made the organization better
- Accomplishment or project you lead that was wonderful
- Award you received for being awesome and exceeding expectations

➢ Infrastructure
- Accomplishment that achieved a lot in a few words but enough so the person reading it gets the idea that you are able to make a strong contribution to improve the company by 10%
- A few more accomplishments related to infrastructure

➢ Technology
- Responsible for network security: designed network security plan, performed advanced firewall/UTM configuration, managed client security/anti-malware services, and achieved annual PCI compliance.
- Created backup/disaster recovery plan with off-site colocation, data replication, and failover.

**ANOTHER COMPANY (Maybe it had a different name earlier)** Cleveland OH          1999 to 2005
*Title (2003 to 2005)*
Lead administrator for in-house graphic arts and interactive production subsidiary of this large regional advertising agency. Supervised junior systems administrator. Assisted CIO with recommendations for capital budgets.
- Created online ad generation tool marketed to clients including Nationwide Insurance. Hskjueliuytbkj  kjuiyiu  kjh kjhiuyir tajk hee giuegr jkh adh iureui yebkjhktyiuy s  defiut kjggeur  jskjdjyur utyia s jdhkr ue ka akjsh df kajhsd uyth.
- Designed, implemented, administered multi-terabyte UNIX and Windows graphic arts servers saving the company 15% on electricity over a two year period.
- Infrastructure and other cool stuff you accomplished in that role; it was really awesome and saved the company a lot of money and time, shocked no one thought of it earlier.

*Title (2000 to 2003)*
An earlier role with this company
- Created online ad generation tool marketed to clients who used tool to grow business by 25% or some sort of other accomplishment that no one else ever thought of before
- Designed, implemented, administered multi-terabyte UNIX and Windows graphic arts servers.
- Infrastructure and other cool stuff you accomplished in that role; it was really awesome

*Title (1999 to 2000)*
- Created online ad generation tool marketed to clients including Nationwide Insurance.
- Designed, implemented, administered multi-terabyte UNIX and Windows graphic arts servers.
- Infrastructure and other cool stuff you accomplished in that role; it was really awesome

# Sample Resume – Page Two

**Your Name, Page two**                                                                                       YName@gmail.com

**XYZ COMPANY  Akron OH**                                                                          1996 to 1999
*Title*
Designed and programmed AdBuilder, an automated ad-production system generating over $15,000 profit per production run. Agency
integrated AdBuilder into AdSuite, its set of proprietary Web applications for managing advertising production and media buying.
- Administered UNIX, Linux, NT, Novell, NeXT servers, Cisco switches.
- Implemented, administered, and provided training for a Digital Asset Management system.
- Supported hardware, software, and users of Mac OS and Windows in large graphic arts production group and rapidly
  growing interactive advertising design and production teams.
- Provided technical support for high-end imagesetters and RIPs.

**ABC PRODUCTION SERVICES  Rockford IL**                                                    1995 to 1996
*Title*
Produced print advertising for clients including American Airlines, NationsBank, Nortel, and Subaru. It was a long time ago so it is not
necessary to write much about this experience. Just enough to show you learned something and maybe contributed.
- Fewer accomplishments are needed the further back in time you go

**FREELANCE GRAPHIC DESIGN/PREPRESS**                                               1993 to 1995
- Provided design, layout, and prepress services to the Federal Reserve Bank, SMU Press, national literary journal *Southwest
  Review*, public relations firms, restaurants, and other clients.

**DALLAS OBSERVER  Dallas TX**                                                                   1991 to 1993
*Copy/Layout Editor*

## TECHNICAL SKILLS

Operating Systems:
- Microsoft Server through 2008R2, Linux, Mac OSX Server

Software / Hardware:
- Active Director / Group Policies, SQL Server, Citrix ZenServer, Wowza Media Server

Languages:
- VBA, Applescript, JavaScript

## EDUCATION

**YOUR UNIVERSITY**  Chicago, IL   B.A. in Linguistics cum Laude

# Discussion Questions

A resume is a very personal document intended for wide distribution. That makes your resume a touchy subject. We can learn a great deal from other people's experiences that we can apply to our own experience.

We encourage you to discuss this book and your resume with others who are having a similar experience. Working together increases camaraderie and leverages the strengths of the individuals across the group. If you are not already a part of a job seekers group, find one in your community and attend regularly. If you are part of a job seekers group, get more active.

Here are some questions to consider about your resume. You might find these questions interesting to discuss with your job seekers group.

1. Reflect on your prior experience with job searching. Identify three ways searching for a job has changed in your lifetime. What techniques did you use in your early year? How has creating a resume

changed since your first job? Contrast your previous efforts with what you know now.

2. Compare your new resume to your old resume. Identify and explain five ways the two resumes are different.

3. We recommend you begin building your resume with on paper although most of your job search will occur on the Internet. Based on your experience completing the activities in this book, how was the paper first process helpful? Identify 3 benefits you found from creating the paper version first.

4. What is your "brand"? When did you begin noticing your reputation? What experiences strengthen your brand? What do you want your brand to stand for? What steps could you take to reinforce a positive brand or adjust a brand to be more positive?

5. How do you plan to share your reputation or brand today? Identify ways you can improve your

brand recognition. -List three actions you can take to do that.

6.  How could you build your LinkedIn profile if you have two career interests? Create a list of actions you can take to make your diverse career interests recognizable on LinkedIn.

7.  Look around LinkedIn to find three of people in your profession who have what you think is a well-done profile. Identify the qualities that effected your impression. Create a list of things you could do to translate the less positive profiles so their message is more like the positive profiles? Use your list to review your own profile to make sure you are creating a positive impression.

8.  Identify three profiles for people in your profession whose information is generic, or not focused on the specific job position they currently hold. Compare those to the strong profiles you identified above. What are the differences you can identify? Which of the identified qualities are in your profile? How can you fix them?

9. Convert your resume to a functional resume. How does this presentation help you identify your strengths and weaknesses? Can you see areas in your functional resume that need to be strengthened? How can you do that?

# References

About.com (2012). How to break into standup comedy. Retrieved from

http://comedians.about.com/od/breakingin/

Breaugh, J.A. (2009). Recruiting and attracting talent: A guide to understanding and managing the recruitment process. Society for Human Resource Management Foundation's Effective Practice Guidelines Series. Retrieved from

http://www.shrm.org/about/foundation/products/Documents/1109%20Recruiting%20EPG-%20Final.pdf

Burke, M.E. (2004). Background checks and resume inaccuracies. Society for Human Resource Management. Retrieved from.

http://www.shrm.org/Research/SurveyFindings/Documents/Reference%20and%20Background%20Checking%20Survey%20Report.pdf

Evans, W. (2012). You have 6 seconds to make an impression: How recruiters see your resume. The

Ladders blog (March 21, 2012). Retrieved from http://blog.theladders.com/ux/you-only-get-6-seconds-of-fame-make-it-count/

Giang, V., & Lockhart, J. (2012). Busted: This is what happened to 10 executives who lied about their resumes. Business Insider, May 7, 2012. Retrieved from http://www.businessinsider.com/9-people-who-were-publicly-shamed-for-lying-on-their-resumes-2012-5?op=1#ixzz2ikuuCrrN

Hastings, R.R. (2012). Resume refresher: Less is more. Society for Human Resource Management (SHRM) Student Focus. Spring, 2012. Retrieved from http://www.shrm.org/communities/studentprograms/documents/shrmstudent%20focus/shrmstudent%20focus%20spring%202011.pdf

Jackman, H. (2012). Get hired: 5 creative ways to rise above the crowd in a job search. World Wide of Work: News and Views of the Working World. Retrieved from http://www.wideworldofwork.com/2012/05/14/

get-hired-5-creative-ways-to-rise-above-the-
crowd-in-a-job-search/

Nemdo, M. (2012). "Are these resume buzzwords kill-
ing your chances? AOL Jobs.com, December 6,
2012. Retrieved from
http://jobs.aol.com/articles/2012/12/06/forget-the-
buzzwords-how-to-create-a-resume-that-sells-you/

*Schepp, D. (2011). Presumes: An unconventional, yet
effective, way to land an interview [Infographic].
AOL Jobs. Retrieved from
http://jobs.aol.com/articles/2011/10/12/presumes-
an-unconventional-yet-effective-way-to-land-an-
inter/*

SHRM Research Spotlight: Which recruiting method is
your organization currently using, November 15,
2005? Retrieved from
http://www.shrm.org/Research/SurveyFindings/Do
cu-
ments/Which_20recruiting_20method_20is_20your
_20organization_20currently_20using_.ppt

Society for Human Resource Management (2005).
Which mistakes have you seen on resumes? SHRM
Weekly Online Survey July 19, 2005. Retrieved
from
http://www.shrm.org/research/surveyfindings/doc
uments/which_20of_20the_20following_20mistakes
_20have_20you_20seen_20on_20resumes_20and_or
_20cover_20letters_.ppt

Society for Human Resource Management (2011). Social networking websites and staffing; Organizations' use of social networking websites for screen-
ing job candidates. SHRMR Research Spotlight. Society for Human Resource Management. Retrieved
from
http://www.shrm.org/Research/SurveyFindings/Ar
ticles/Documents/PART%202_Social%20Media%20
Flier_FINAL.pdf

Society for Human Resource Management, (2011). Social networking websites and staffing:. SHRM Research Spotlight. Society for Human Resource
Management, April 2011. Retrieved from
http://www.shrm.org/Research/SurveyFindings/Do

144

cu-
ments/Social%20Networking%20Flyer_Staffing%20
Conference_FINAL1.pdf

Society for Human Resource Management,. (2004). Resume inaccuracies and hiring. Society for Human
Resource Management. Retrieved from
https://www.google.com/url?sa=t&rct=j&q=&esrc=s
&source=web&cd=1&ved=0CDQQFjAA&url=http
%3A%2F%2Fwww.shrm.org%2FResearch%2FSurv
eyFind-
ings%2FDocuments%2FHow_20important_20are_2
0inaccuracies_20in_20resumes_20on_20your_20dec
ision_20to_20hire_.ppt&ei=qUzkUMC6EoeW8gTK
n4CQBA&usg=AFQjCNHlfyulbLquvuT-
SsOuoJ__N7w42w&sig2=dKX_Ry3OkF5fxE5f2kD5
pw

Statistics Brain, (2012). Resume Falsification Statistics.
Statistics Brain, July 16, 2012. Retrieved from
http://www.statisticbrain.com/resume-falsification-
statistics/

## About The Interview Doctor, Inc. ®

Do the stories in this book sound familiar? Have you been in the same position as these people looking for a job? Are you at your wits end?

The Interview Doctor® can show you a better way.

The Interview Doctor® can save you time and effort, moving your job search ahead by miles so you can land the job you love. We have the insight because we have the personal experience finding jobs and the business experience hiring people. We know how you feel. We know what employers are looking for. We know how to break through those barriers with the right techniques to get the job you love.

We coach candidates via phone or in person - our services are available when and where you need them.

Shorten your job search. Find the job you love. Get the answers you need with personal job search coaching from The Interview Doctor®.

Become the one of the success stories. Working with The Interview Doctor® you will see results!

- Know your story and how to use it to get a job offer

- Know the important pieces to include in your resume

- Break through the Phone Screen barrier and land the job interview

- Understand how to act and what to say in the actual interview

All of these pieces play an important part in landing the job offer. When you go through our Job Interview Coaching process you will learn how to adjust your job search tactics and improve your results – resulting in Job Offers and landing the Job you love.

Contact The Interview Doctor® and get the help you need with your Job Interview and Search.

**Katherine Burik** is an energetic and creative leader with a service focus to human resources. She has specific expertise in strategic human resource planning and coaching leadership teams to improve performance and results.

The Interview Doctor sprang from Katherine's observation, based on her human resource experience and work with recruiters that candidates need to improve their interviewing skills. She coaches candidates looking for jobs, and speaks frequently to groups about career development and successful job search techniques. Her thoughts about job search appear regularly in The Interview Doctor blog.

In her previous life as Vice President or Director of Human Resources at several businesses in Chicago and Northeast Ohio, Katherine reported to the President and CEO, responsible for the entire array of human resource functions. She has been laid off more times than most people she knows. Contrary to public opinion, being laid off can be liberating!

Katherine is a member of the Society of Human Resource Managers, the American Society of Training and Development, and the Worldwide Association of Business Coaches.

She earned her BA in History from Northwestern University and MS in Industrial Relations from Loyola University of Chicago. She has been certified as a Senior HR Professional by the Society of Human Resource

Managers and is certified as a Registered Corporate Coach.

**Dan Toussant** is a human resource professional with over 20 years of leadership experience, specializing in management and professional recruiting. He speaks regularly to groups about the job-seeking process, and coaches professionals of any age one-on-one regarding interviewing skills, resume preparation, and career transition. He serves as the co-editor of The Interview Doctor Blog, and teams with his business partner, Katherine Burik, and other HR professionals in this job-interviewing skills, career-coaching collaborative, The Interview Doctor.

Dan holds a master's degree in Education from Kent State University and a Bachelor's degree in English from Boston College.

He is the beneficiary of some rather unique job promotions and changes in his professional life. Staying in his hometown and still working to advance his career has led to some interesting opportunities including nine years as HR Consulting Leader with a regional CPA firm, and now as a Professional Recruiter and Job-Interviewing-Skills Webinar/Seminar Presenter and Coach.

He is an active member of Toastmasters International, Business Networking International (BNI), and the Society of Human Resource Management.

**Connect with us:** We want to connect with you on LinkedIn individually and at our LinkedIn Group, Job Search Check-Up. See how our contacts can help you in your job search!

Call the Interview Doctor® today at 800-914-7349! Sign up to receive our newsletter and blog at http://jobinterviewcoaching.org/contact/.

# Read on for a Preview of next book in The Job Seeker Manifesto series!

## The Job Seeker Manifesto

*"Tell Me About Yourself...":*

*The Secret to Getting Your Next Job!*

By

**Katherine Burik**

**The Interview Doctor®**

# "Tell me about yourself"...:
# The Secret to Getting Your Next Job

## How is comedy like an interview?

The old joke starts, "A guy walks into a bar." This opening alerts the listener that something funny is supposed to happen next. This joke has many variations. You can change the joke around all sorts of ways to make it different than the last time.

Consider these oldies but goodies:

- A fish walks into a bar. The bartender says, "What do you want?" The fish croaks, "Water".

- A grasshopper walks into a bar. The barman looks at him and says, "Did you know there is a drink named after you?" "Really?" says the grasshopper. "There's a drink called Herman?"

- A priest, a rabbi, and a vicar walk into a pub. The barman says, "Is this some kind of a joke?"

Funny, huh?

Every joke has a formula. There is the opening line, an observation about the character or the situation, then the punch line. Sometimes it is a long rambling story and sometimes it is a short, to the point joke. The combination of factors inside the joke makes it funny even though you know the joke is a formula. The formula gives structure and leads the listener from the opening to a point at the end, which is the laugh.

Comedians are expert storytellers. They appear so natural when you see them on TV or in concert. They stand up at the microphone and talk to the audience. They tell stories and jokes smoothly and with a purpose. You do not see all the preparation that went into making the joke come out funny at the end of the formula. You do not see all the hours spent practicing. The good ones are so confident. It seems like they are talking directly to you. You like them and want them to succeed.

Not every comedian is funny just as not every storyteller can really tell a good story.

It is hard to put your finger on what might be missing, but something is missing. There are usually some visible signs. New comedians or bad ones are often not confident. They sweat a lot and stammer. The jokes have no structure and nothing is funny. They do not really have anything to say. They just blather on. You feel bad for them but you know you do not want to see them again.

I cannot tell jokes well at all. Even stories are a little beyond me. I can hear it in my head but when I open my mouth, it comes out all wrong. Listeners sit there waiting for the punch line, disappointed when it comes out all wrong.

### An interview is a formula too

What does joke telling have to do with interviewing? More than you think. Stay with me on this.

An interview is a formula with many different combinations. It invariably starts with, "Tell me about yourself". Where it goes from there often depends on you.

Candidates who interview well are confident and smooth. They have a story to tell and they tell it well. They use stories to draw a connection between what they have done and what they want. You like them and want them to be successful.

Candidates who interview poorly do not have much to say. They stammer and sweat, seldom making eye contact because they lack confidence. They talk but all you hear is blah, blah, blah. They do not clearly communicate what they want or why they should have it. You want them out of your office as fast as possible. You feel bad for them but you know you do not want to see them again.

Just like bad comedians, it is hard to put your finger on what is wrong but something is missing.

If you look closely, what is missing is structure. A poor interviewer, like a bad comedian, has not considered the structure behind the stories, he has not practiced enough beforehand, and usually does not really know what he wants out of the interview.

The formula behind a good joke or a good story is a structure that adds discipline. Just as structure and discipline ensures that the joke or story comes out the way the teller intends, discipline of preparation and structure is important to an interview. You might not be aware of how important it is to making you feel confident in everything you do.

It is a circle. Structuring your presentation (joke, story, or interview) requires discipline. Discipline means preparation. Preparation leads to confidence. Confidence brings the audience through the structure to the punch line!

**Ten Tips for Beginners**

Being a great comedian or interviewer takes a great deal of practice. These ten tips for beginning stand-up comedians can also help candidates preparing to interview for a job (About.com).

1.  **Get on stage now.** Practice your interview responses as often as you can in front of real people. The more you practice, the more natural you will sound.

Never pass up a chance to talk to someone about your background and what you want. Always be prepared to talk about yourself and your goals. You never know when the opportunity will strike but take advantage of every one.

At a recent dinner party, I was seated next to someone I did not know. She asked questions about what I did. Because I was prepared to answer, a simple dinner party turned into a discussion about The Interview Doctor and how we have fast action remedies for people searching for jobs. It was a chance for me to practice talking about what I do and who I am.

If I stammered and stuttered like a bad candidate or a bad comedian, she would have turned away. She only listened because I fluently told my story. My story had a beginning, middle, and an end. Get out and talk about yourself as often as you can.

2.  **Do not be afraid to bomb.** Your responses to an interview never come out of your mouth the way you intend unless to say it aloud a lot. Practice is

critical. The first few times you say your responses aloud you will sound silly even to yourself. You may bomb. However, you will get better over time.

3. **Keep up with your old stuff.** There is always room for improvement in your responses. Practice your tried and true responses along with responses to new questions you heard or are trying out. Critique your past performances and identify areas for improvement.

4. **Do not steal or even borrow.** Like comedians, we never ever tell a lie or even exaggerate about our background. It is not worth it. It always ends in trouble, sometimes legal trouble. Be proud of your background. If you are not proud of what you have done, how can a company take you seriously?

5. **Stick to your time.** Do not babble in interviews or in conversations with people you meet. Be respectful of time. Tell your story clearly and succinctly. Then be quiet. Be on time. End meetings on time.

6. **Tape yourself.** This is great advice for candidates. Make sure you like the way you sound and that the way you sound and look represents the person you want the employer to see. Make direct eye contact. Be aware of your image. Be purposeful in selecting the clothes you wear, your personal grooming, and mannerisms. Do not take chances. Taping yourself gives insight you will not get any other way.

7. **Hit the clubs.** Get out and meet people. Get your name out there. Networking at meetings and with people you meet leads to opportunities you would not find sitting in your basement office

8. **Make nice with the audience.** Be friendly and open so people you meet will like you. Be nice to everyone including the receptionist and the janitor. Companies hire people they like who they think will fit in with the other folks. Be the person they like.

9. **Carry a notebook with you.** You never know when you will need to write something down so be pre-pared, be aware, and take notes to review later. A

notebook is a great place to record observations about your job search that strike you when you are out and about. It also is a convenient prop if you are stuck waiting for someone. You can always look busy.

10. **Be yourself.** Let people see the real you. Be genuine. Relax. Let your preparation make you confident. Breathe.

## Preparation is the key

The common denominator between comedians and interviewing is preparation. Being prepared makes you confident so you can be yourself and be the person the hiring manager likes and wants to hire.

In our recruiting experience, we met many sad, poor candidates. These folks had nice backgrounds on paper or they would not have been invited in for an interview. However, their presentation in person was poor. They did not know what to say. They could not describe their background. They did not have a story to tell. Needless to say, these folks were not hired.

I have changed jobs many times, more often than I like to talk about. I am a quiet person. I find it difficult to talk off the cuff. Meeting new people sometimes scares me to the core. I stammer and stutter while I am forming a good response. Interviews are the forum for quick talking, flashy folks, and not quiet folks like me.

The first few times I was laid off I was out of work for a long time. I did not know how to network. I was shy and quiet. I had trouble talking about myself. I stammered through interviews because I did not know what to say. My search process lacked discipline and my approach to interviews lacked structure. I needed to figure out a better way.

I did some deep soul searching about the interview process and about my performance. I realized that most interviews followed a pattern. Most hiring managers I spoke to asked the same questions. That gave me an idea.

If I prepared my answers in advance and practiced, I might be more comfortable. Being more comfortable might help me express myself better during interviews.

I did not want to mess up any more interviews so I tried an experiment in a low risk situation at a few parties where I did not know many people. Before the party, I read the Wall Street Journal and picked out about five or six topics I thought might come up in conversation. Then I walked up someone I did not know and brought up one of the topics I prepared. To my surprise, the person responded! It sparked a conversation that I could handle because I did the research ahead of time. I felt more confident and the people I met seemed to respond positively to me.

I needed to try it next in interviews. I found all the possible questions I thought I might be asked and wrote answers to all of them. I said my answers aloud looking in the mirror. I changed my self-talk from, "who do you think you are?" to "Ok, I can do this". At the next interview, I repeated the answers I prepared and rehearsed in advance.

It worked! I was more relaxed. The words flowed out just as I practiced. I answered the questions well without stammering since I knew what I wanted to say. Moreover, the hiring managers liked me! I got a job!

I personally used this approach for the last 30 years in my own career. This approach works for many clients at The Interview Doctor. It can work for you!

This book describes the special Interview Doctor techniques for being prepared to answer the foundational interviewing question, "Tell Me about Yourself". Let us get started.

# What does a bad interview sound like?

Good preparation begins with facing the truth. What do you really sound like in an interview? We have interviewed thousands of people. We can tell the difference between a good interview and a bad interview. But can you?

If you have had more than a few interviews but never get the job offer, you are probably doing something wrong during the interview. Until you figure out what you are doing wrong, you will not be able to improve.

Listen to this interview and consider whether you would hire Sandy:

*Interviewer:* Good morning. I am glad you could come in today. Tell me a little about yourself.

*Sandy: [quiet, head down, no eye contact, very soft]*

Well, I work in accounting. *[Long pause]*

*Interviewer:* Uh huh. Tell me a little more.

*Sandy: [still quiet, not making eye contact, head down but starts talking]*

I am not sure what else you want to know. It has been a roundabout path to get here. I grew up in a small town in Ohio. I got my high school girl friend pregnant so we got married. We have two kids together but the marriage never really worked. So I left her. I really miss my kids. They live in Wisconsin now. I had to move to Cleveland to find work.

I really miss my kids. My youngest, Tom, is severely autistic so he needs special care, which is expensive. His behavior is really awful. We can't take him anywhere.

I've held a bunch of bad jobs. I never seem to stay very long at any one thing. A friend told me about this program so I decided to get some extra training while I am out of work.

I really miss my kids. I wish I could see them more often but it takes a lot of hours to work in accounting, especially during the monthly close so I do not have a lot of time.

PAUSE   I am not sure what else you want to know

*Interviewer:* Why do you want to leave your job?

*Sandy:  [starts getting louder and kind of obnoxious, finally makes a little eye contact]*

My last job was awful. The boss was a real jerk. Everyone hated him. I was there for about 4 months when he yelled at me in front of the group for putting this charge in the wrong account again. He was unreasonable too. He expected me to work at all hours and do all this stupid grunt work. The rules were stupid too.

The last straw was when he told me to come in to work on Labor Day to finish the close but I already told him I was planning to go to Wisconsin to see the kids for the weekend. I really gave it to him. I told him what he could do with his stupid job and then I walked out.

*Interviewer:* Mmmm… ok, what kind of position are you looking for now?

*Sandy:* I really need a position that pays well. I am behind in so many bills. I am about to be evicted if I do not get a good paying job right now, not to mention my son's medical bills. I would like to find a place where I can work for the rest of my life.

*Interviewer:* Why should we hire you?

*Sandy: [Pauses]* I am not sure really. My friend told me to come here today. *[Pauses again]* What kinds of positions do you have open right now?

**Who Would You Hire?**

What is going through the interviewer's mind at the end of this exchange? If you were the interviewer, would you offer Sandy a job? Probably not. I would not. No one will.

Want to read more? Check your bookseller for The Interview Doctor's next installment of The Job Seeker Manifesto:

## *"Tell Me About Yourself..."*:

### *The Secret to Getting Your Next Job!*

**By**

**Katherine Burik**

**The Interview Doctor®**

# Coming Soon!